The Forest and the Trees

The Forest and the Trees
Helping Teachers Integrate a Biblical Worldview Across the Curriculum

RICHARD A. WIDDER
AND WENDY WIDDER

WIPF & STOCK · Eugene, Oregon

THE FOREST AND THE TREES
Helping Teachers Integrate a Biblical Worldview Across the Curriculum

Copyright © 2008 Richard A. Widder and Wendy Widder. All rights reserved. Except for brief quotations in critical publications or reviews, no part of this book may be reproduced in any manner without prior written permission from the publisher. Write: Permissions, Wipf and Stock, 199 W. 8th Ave., Suite 3, Eugene, OR 97401.

www.wipfandstock.com
ISBN 13: 978-1-55635-054-2

Manufactured in the U.S.A.

All Scripture quotations, unless otherwise indicated, are from the *Holy Bible, New International Version*®. Copyright © 1973, 1978, 1984 by International Bible Society. Used by permission of Zondervan. All rights reserved.

Scripture quotations marked KJV are from the King James Version.

To Christian Teachers
who have the ongoing task of integrating their subject matter
with the truth of God's Word.

———————— Contents ————————

Preface / ix

Introduction / 1

1 • Nature / 11

2 • People / 36

3 • Communication / 62

4 • Beauty / 89

5 • Ultimate Issues / 114

Conclusion / 136

Bibliography / 139

Preface

Ask nearly any elementary student what their favorite school subject is, and the likely answer is "recess" or "gym." Ask a middle or high school student the same question and the answer may come back, "lunch" or "study hall." Recess, snow days, and summer vacation are greeted with shouts of joy, while having to go to school and do homework are viewed as drudgery and punishment by a frightening percentage of students.

We do not mean to paint a dreary picture of the classroom (truth be told, we've cheered on snowy mornings when school has been cancelled), but having spent a combined fifty years in the elementary classroom, middle and high school administration, and school board service, we are confident you understand what we're talking about.

"Why do we have to learn this?" moan students when the topic at hand is less than interesting to them. Teachers generally answer this maddening question in one of two ways: waxing eloquent about why the study of square roots is a critical exercise or simply trying to silence the questioner with a response like "because it's good for you," or "you'll need it when you grow up," or (on more frustrating days) "because I said so."

If you think about it, though, it's a great question. What *is* the point? What is the value of knowing what integers, linking verbs, and ionic bonds are? Why do we think students need to learn the dates of the American Civil War, the structure of haiku, and the literary themes in *Romeo and Juliet*? What do these things have to do with the everyday lives our students lead?

We may as well admit it—many of the things we teach have little or nothing to do with the everyday lives of our students, both now and in the future when they become adults. This does not mean, of course, that we should excise them from our curriculum, because you know as well as we do that the process of learning is as important—and sometimes even more important—than the actual content. Through the schooling process, students learn facts and skills that hone their interests, but more importantly, they develop a set of values through which they see the world.

Preface

As our students journey through elementary and secondary education, they develop, without even realizing it, a worldview that influences every decision they will make as adults.

In light of this, an even better question for Christian school teachers is, "What worldview am I shaping in my students by what I teach?" What makes Christian education any different from its non-Christian counterparts?

In theory, at least, the hallmark of Christian education is the integration of the Word of God and the God of the Word with all academic areas. There was a time in our country when education and the Christian faith stood side by side in the classroom. God was the Creator, and students of the natural world marveled at His vast wisdom in its design and operation. Every subject area was permeated by the Judeo-Christian worldview, which provided a Christian focus to our understanding of man and his world.

But times have changed, and rather than God being honored as Creator and the source of all wisdom, human reason is believed to be completely adequate for discovering the secrets of the physical world and solving all the problems of humankind.

Out of this cultural shift arose Christian schools, seeking to preserve the Christian worldview in the upcoming generations by teaching a unified view of truth—God's truth. In the Christian school, secular knowledge should be as sacred as sacred knowledge because both are part of God's massive body of truths that fill this universe. All truth is God's truth.

Students receive an education of sorts in *every* Christian school when they learn to read, write, solve mathematical problems, study the natural world, and understand how people live together as families, communities, and nations. But if students do not also learn how each of these vital areas flows from the Word of God and how each is related to God, we are just teaching truth, and not God. The Christian school must do both simultaneously.

This monumental task has been helped, in part, by Christian publishers who have taken up the challenge of producing materials from within a Christian worldview. Such materials provide an alternative to the secular publishers' curricular materials that are devoid of Christian content and truth.

But while these Christian textbooks have helped meet an urgent need, they are not enough because the greatest influence on the worldviews of the next generation is the worldview of those who instruct them. Your ability as teachers to integrate the truths of God's Word with every facet of the curriculum, regardless of what textbooks you use, is what guarantees or jeopardizes the possibility that your students will receive a truly Christian education. Teachers, beginning in the kindergarten classroom and going all the way through high school graduation, carry the heaviest responsibility for the primary task of the Christian school—day-by-day, subject-by-subject integration of curricular material and biblical truth.

It all sounds great, doesn't it? But we know better. We know that in the flurry of classroom activity, you are often happy just to get through the day's lesson. We know that when you are turning somersaults to meet ever-increasing standardization requirements, the thought of trying to meet one more expectation is overwhelming. We know that in the normal classroom the forest gets easily lost for all the trees that are growing there.

This book is to help you see the forest again, or perhaps for the first time. We want to help you understand how God's truth, His bigger Story, shapes every aspect of what your textbooks contain. And we want to gently help you understand that if you fail to integrate everything you teach with that Story, you fail to teach Christianly.[1]

In short, we want to give you a better answer for the question, "Why do we have to learn this?" that students ask, and for the question, "What worldview am I shaping in my students by what I teach?" that you should be asking every time you stand in front of your class. To accomplish this, we will walk through the pages of God's Story and help you see how each subject you teach flows from these pages. This book is meant to be comprehensive, but at the same time, it is only the beginning of what we hope will be an exciting career-long journey you take with your students.

---

1. Our use of the word "Story" in no way implies that the Bible is myth or fictional. Rather, we use the term to acknowledge the fact that God has revealed Himself through an intricately told, historically true Story. When He determined what He wanted us to know about Him, He didn't write a history book, an itemized list of attributes, or a "facts-n-figures" book. Instead, He wove together hundreds of events into a compelling story, complete with characters, tension, setting, plot, climax, and everything else that makes a good story. We capitalize the word *story* because it is the ultimate Story into which all others must fit.

Introduction

At the Christian school where we have invested a significant portion of our lives, the annual high school commencement exercises include a sort of "who's who" when diplomas are awarded. As the graduates make their way across the platform, the superintendent reads each student's name, identifies his or her parents, and announces what the student's post-graduation plans are, complete with scholarship awards and career goals. This nice gesture is the school's way of honoring the graduates, but it also sends a subtle message to the audience that the school has succeeded as an educational institution.

This annual order of events could just as easily be done—and probably is—in many non-Christian school ceremonies as well, because all traditional schools have the same general purpose. Regardless of religious affiliation, schools exist to help parents raise up the next generation to take its place in the world. From the first frightening days of kindergarten, students are guided through the step-by-step, skill-by-skill process of becoming adults. When a school finally sends its students out the door and into the world, mortarboards in hand, it hopes they are equipped to move with skill and purpose into respectable, responsible adulthood.

Accomplishing this goal requires that schools help children, preteens, and young adults work through two critical questions that have haunted humans for as long as anyone can remember—"Who am I?" and "Why am I here?" Without an adequate understanding of their identity and reason for existence, graduates will flounder in purposelessness and find their diplomas insufficient to meet the challenges of adult life.

However, while Christian and non-Christian schools may share this overarching goal, the answers each brings to these questions come from two drastically different worldviews. In these dissimilar worldviews lies the primary difference between Christian and non-Christian schools.

Two Worldviews—Naturalism and Theism

Certainly there are more than two ways to look at the world. We live in a world torn apart by conflicting ideas and beliefs. However, since we suspect you are not interested in a serious philosophical discussion of an array of worldviews, we are only going to look at the two most relevant to our discussion. (Flatter your school's philosophy teacher by asking for a one-day seminar on the smorgasbord of available worldviews, or check out *The Universe Next Door* by James Sire, listed in the additional resources at the end of chapter 5.) The ideas and beliefs of each worldview infiltrate everything that happens in the classroom—whether or not the teacher is aware of it.

The first worldview we want to consider is naturalism, the value system that has dominated our culture for the past number of centuries and has fathered many other worldviews. The second worldview is theism, the opposing set of values that Christians have—or, as the point of this book is, *should* have. Let's consider an analogy that can hopefully define the basics of these worldviews.

Think about the goldfish that lives in a small glass bowl at the back of your classroom. If you don't have a goldfish, imagine that you do. His immediate surroundings may be confining, but he can see beyond the edges of his bowl into the vast unknown of your classroom. He sees shapes and colors (unless goldfish are colorblind) and movement.

If your goldfish happens to be a *naturalist*, the universe of your classroom is all there is. It is a universe governed by laws (mostly yours) and patterns. Lots of things happen within it that he can observe from his bowl (and who really knows what he does after hours when the classroom is dark and empty). He has observed countless things that require explanation. For example, every morning people of varying sizes appear. He's not sure how they get there, or what happens to them when the clock strikes three, but as a naturalist, his theory is that something in the environment of the classroom accounts for both their existence and their daily disappearance, because everything that exists does so within the confines of your classroom. To the naturalist goldfish, your classroom is what we call a "closed system": nothing exists outside of it, and everything within it has to be explained using the laws and patterns of your classroom.

The *theist* goldfish, on the other hand, may believe that your classroom is the universe, but he does not believe it is all there is. The "natural world" of your classroom may be governed by laws and patterns, but it is not a closed system. Instead it is an "open system," meaning that there are forces beyond the confines of the classroom universe that dictate an awful lot of what happens in it—events for which your goldfish can find no natural explanation. Like what happened to Suzy's missing homework when she says the dog ate it, why Johnny always appears twenty minutes later than everyone else, and why everyone groans when the talking box on the wall says fish sticks are for lunch (hopefully not goldfish sticks). Because he believes forces not only exist outside the natural world of your classroom but they can also affect what actually happens inside it, he recognizes the "super"-natural—that is, those forces that transcend natural laws. God, of course, represents these supernatural "forces" in the theistic worldview.

While overly simplistic and obviously flawed, this analogy captures the essence of the chasm between naturalism and Christian theism: the existence and relevance of God. For the naturalist in his closed system, the existence of some transcendent Being is not even a question to be considered. And if perchance a "god" did exist, he would be irrelevant because he exists outside the system and is unable to penetrate it. As the highest life form in the "system," humans have all the necessary equipment to solve the questions of life, from the mundane to the ultimate. At the heart of naturalism is the human person; essentially, the human *is* god.

At the heart of Christian theism, on the other hand, is the transcendent God who is the Creator and Sustainer of life, both in the universe we know and in whatever may exist outside it. Nature, as we understand it, is controlled by what we call the laws of nature—those predictable, knowable factors that help us come to grips with how things work—but for the theist, the natural boundaries of the universe are not the ultimate boundaries. God is. Not only *can* He affect life inside our system, He continually *does*. The natural world we know is forever dependent on His provision and sustenance of life. He is the absolute sovereign of all that is.

The Dangerous Dominance of Naturalism

Although the thrust of this book is helping you understand how the theistic worldview relates to education, it is important that we first understand how naturalism dominates our cultural landscape. Naturalism is the driving force behind philosophies, theories of science, views of truth, theories of origins, moral values, and ultimate issues that we bump into every day. In the field of education, this means teacher training programs, textbook writing, and educational theories and policies all bow to the no-god bias of naturalism. We are not safe from its power even within the walls of our Christian schools with Christian books, praying parents, godly administrators, and devout board members.

Naturalism confronts us at every turn: the news media, legislative actions, cultural issues, the courts, the entertainment industry, music, art, and literature. This steady, but often silent, exposure to naturalism's values influences everything we do. The same is true for our students—yet, for them, it is even more dangerous because they have not developed the wherewithal to discern the crucial differences between naturalism and theism. They come to school nourished by a daily diet of naturalism's tenets, served on the platters of television, movies, video games, and Internet access, to name a few. Even our finest students from the best Christian families have naturalism's nutrients feeding their minds and spirits.

In their book *How Now Shall We Live?* Charles Colson and Nancy Pearcey contrast the five key tenets of naturalism with the opposing tenets of theism.[1] We have adapted their list for our purposes on the next page.

Sacred and Secular—The Great Divide

These contrasting tenets lie behind the familiar distinction made between things that are "sacred" and those that are "secular." In general, people consider something sacred if it is connected to God (or a "god") or has some religious purpose, while something is considered secular if it has no connection to or concern with religion.

While such a divide is appropriate at times (e.g., "Holy, Holy, Holy" is definitely a "sacred" song that very much relates truth about God, while "Row, Row, Row Your Boat" does not), such a sharp dichotomy has conditioned our culture to believe that sacred and secular represent two exclusive, opposed, and contradictory groups. Additionally, abuse of the idea of "separation of church and state" has pitted each against the other in the public square. Thus, naturalists and Christian theists across this fine country wage war over the display of the Ten Commandments in public places, the presence of nativity scenes on city property, and even the classroom recitation of the Pledge of Allegiance. This pervasive division has increasingly forced God out of culture and enthroned humans as the Ultimate Beings; naturalism (also known as secular humanism) reigns as the "religion" of the day, and it wants nothing to do with Christian theism.

In spite of naturalism's claim to separate sacred from secular, it is important to understand that naturalism will, in fact, tolerate an immense amount of "sacred" in its policies and procedures—as long as it's not *Christian* sacredness. Naturalism will tolerate—nay, promote!—Islam, Buddhism, Wicca, and the like because it values a multiculturalism where everyone's values and beliefs are equal (see *multiculturalism* in table).

---

[1]. Colson and Pearcey, *How Now Shall We Live?* 20–21.

Introduction

Naturalism's Basic Beliefs	Theism's Response
Moral relativism: "If it feels good, do it." Each person or society creates its own moral truth, based on personal preferences.	God has given standards of right and wrong that are absolute.
Multiculturalism: "I'm okay; you're okay." The histories and values of each culture are morally equal; no one culture or belief system can make any claims of having the truth.	God's standard of truth speaks to all cultures and is used to judge cultural values as being right or wrong.
Pragmatism: "Whatever works." Policies and values are created on the basis of whatever works for the greatest good.	Policies and values are judged and determined by objective standards from God's Word.
Utopianism: "People are basically good." Human nature is essentially good; with the right economic and social structures people will live in peace and harmony.	Sin is real and has infected the human natures of all people. Laws are necessary to contain human sinfulness and natural tendencies to choose evil over good.
A "this-world" perspective: "Go for the gusto!" This life is all there is.	Life goes on. How we live during our brief time here determines our eternal future.

Learning about other religions becomes a cultural necessity because that is how we learn what others value and how we demonstrate respect for their beliefs. Christianity, however, falls into a different category altogether and naturalism refuses to tolerate expressions of it because, unlike other religions, Christianity teaches that Jesus is the *only* way of salvation, and we do not accept the truth claims of other religions. In reality, it is not the sacred or "spiritual," per se, that is offensive to naturalism. Jesus is offensive. Anything remotely related to this exclusivist Christian religion must be kept separate from all other cultural activity.

For those of us whose lives are defined by Christianity and its sacred beliefs, this is of enormous concern. The attempt to remove physical representations of Christ-related things from every cranny of culture reflects a deeper threat: the desire to obliterate the immaterial effects of Christianity and silence the voice of Christians. Naturalism's refusal to tolerate Christianity in mainstream culture makes it exceedingly difficult for the Christian worldview to influence politics, governments, economics, education, science, and every other discipline at every level. Christian theism and its sacred elements are the enemy.

Blurring the Lines

Given this state of current affairs, what are Christians to do? Perhaps we should just abandon the "secular" altogether and simply urge our children into "full-time Christian ministry." Perhaps we should fight meaner and harder, teaching our children to serve prison sentences valiantly on behalf of "sacred" things we don't want removed from public view. Perhaps we should all move to an island in the South Pacific and wait for Jesus to return.

Or perhaps there is a better way to do battle for the survival of Christian theism in the West and its influence on the world around us.

At the frontlines of this battle stand Christian schools, side by side with the parents they represent. We suggest that one of the most important weapons in the warfare is a better understanding and application of the Christian worldview. When we truly see the world through the theistic worldview, we will also begin to understand that the division between sacred and secular is actually false. All truth is God's truth, a fact that blurs the lines between what is considered "sacred" and what is called "secular." The world is His. If God is the Creator and Sustainer of all life, then everything, by definition, is sacred. Everything is related to Him, and everything matters to Him. He made it all; He keeps it all. Math is a sacred study. Science is the study of God. Art reflects God.

The Christian worldview cultivates a mindset that closes the gap between the secular and the sacred by understanding that there should not be the hard and fast distinctions that we have long accepted. It is, admittedly, difficult for us to blur these lines because we have lived so long with the division. Historically, however, the word *secular* has not meant that something is necessarily opposed to God—the view so many have today. Rather, it has been a positive word in the Christian's vocabulary. R. C. Sproul summarizes the perspective the church has had:

> The church has always had a good view of that which was regarded as secular. In the Middle Ages, for example, men were ordained to a specific role in the priesthood that was called the "secular priesthood." These were men who had responsibilities which took them out of the institution of the church to minister in the world where there were specific needs requiring the healing touch or the priestly ministry of the church. The word *secular* has its origins and its roots in the Latin language and comes from the word *saeculum* which means "world." The secular priest is one who ministers in the world.[2]

We do not deny that the "secular" contains many elements that are blatantly opposed to God—but ironically even those things are sustained and allowed to exist by Him. Neither do we suggest that because everything draws sustenance from Him that everything is good. What we do contend, however, is that the theistic worldview provides a window through which our students can see *everything*—"sacred" and "secular"—as it relates to God; they can come to deeper knowledge of Him as they study every subject we teach in school. When they see the world this way, they will better understand how they fit in the messy picture that is our world.

Christian schools, then, need to help parents raise young people who can be God's messengers, His "secular priests" living and ministering in His world.

The Big Picture

Blurring the lines between sacred and secular requires that we view all aspects of culture within the biblical framework of God's Story as detailed from Genesis to Revelation. Unfortunately, for many of our students—and, sadly, for many of us—the Bible seems quaint and almost obsolete.

2. Sproul, *Lifeviews*, 32–33.

It has lost out in the cultural warfare, and efforts to change this notion in the hearts and minds of our students will be more difficult than swimming upstream against a mighty current. Such change is only even remotely possible when we ensure that our own worldview is thoroughly theistic.

Our goal is to ensure just this by providing you with a unified picture of God's grand Story as revealed in Scripture and by combining the so-called sacred and secular into one worldview. To this end, we have organized the primary academic areas under five broad and often overlapping categories: nature, people, communication, beauty, and ultimate issues. An overview of these five categories and the subject areas they include is listed below:

- *Nature* (science, mathematics, physical education, health): St. Augustine, the premier theologian of the early church, said that "wherever we turn among the things which [God] created and conserved so wonderfully, we discover His footprints, whether lightly or plainly impressed."[3] The study of the natural world allows us to walk in God's footprints.

- *People* (social sciences): God has created human beings in His own image to be people with a variety of relationships. In this second category, we will reflect on what it means to be human by taking a look at our God-ordained relationships.

- *Communication* (language arts, languages, speech): God has revealed Himself through the building block of all language—the Word, both written in the Scriptures and living in the person of Jesus Christ. Developing abilities in language not only enriches our lives, but is fundamental to understanding God Himself . . . and sharing Him with others.

- *Beauty* (music, visual arts, drama): God did not merely make a functional world; He made a beautiful one, filled with diversity and intrigue. Likewise, He has instilled in humans creative desires and abilities to express in many ways, each way unique to the individual and to the culture in which it finds expression. A study of beauty teaches us to better appreciate God Himself, as well as how to use our artistic abilities for the enjoyment of others.

- *Ultimate Issues* (philosophy, religion, Bible, theology): This fifth category is perhaps the area where we currently do the best job of integration because we readily understand how God has made provision for the significant and basic questions of eternity. As we learn about the

3. Augustine, *City of God*, 3.11.28.

Creator-God and about Jesus who died as the punishment for our sins, we come to know God and what He expects from us.

Each chapter concludes with a summary of the truths covered in the chapter for quick reference, a set of teacher tips, and a list of additional resources. The teacher tips may or may not be helpful for your situation, but hopefully they can serve as idea-starters as you work toward integration across the curriculum. The resource lists are minimal: books and materials in each subject area, as you know, are voluminous in quantity; there is no way we can do justice to what is available. What we have tried to do is provide a sampling of resources intended to get you started and keep you exploring, particularly in areas of the curriculum that may not be your specialty. The materials are also varied, and our inclusion of them is not an endorsement of everything contained in the books/videos; we offer them as tools to help you think and to acquaint you with some of the issues that may intersect with your curriculum.

In the conclusion of the book, we offer a helpful tool for thinking through integration in specific disciplines, with the hope that you will begin the practical process and continue it as long as you teach.

Conclusion

We suggested at the beginning of this introduction that our Christian school, like every other school, measures its success in part by the graduates it sends into the community—young adults with a strong sense of who they are and how they fit in the world. What we did not say is that although these are the essential issues that drive every educational institution, answering them adequately is only possible when a school educates through the grid of a thoroughly Christian worldview.

This worldview begins with the most fundamental questions of all: Who is God and what is He like? Students cannot begin to know who they are and where they fit in the world until they come to know their Creator in every facet of life. *This* is the uniqueness of Christian education, and it is hopefully what we parade across the platform every spring. The Christian school has succeeded when it integrates God's truth so well in its subject matter and through the lives of its teachers, staff, and administration that its students understand who they are because they understand whose they are. And they know how they fit in the world because they know whose world it is.

I

Nature

Teaching science in the elementary grades is a little like trying to run the ocean through a sieve by cupfuls. Our youngest students read, discuss, and experiment with a little bit of everything in the natural world—they plant bean seeds in Styrofoam cups, follow the life and times of a classroom pet, construct models of the solar system, and collect rocks from gravel parking lots.

Somewhere in the middle of these hands-on encounters with the natural world, teachers hope their students begin to understand that everything in the world is connected. The sprouting plant in the Styrofoam cup needs the sun from the model to grow, and the pet rabbit would like nothing more than to nibble off the ends of the leggy plant. If the bean plant avoids the rabbit and manages to produce a bean or two, someday even the student could eat it. (The same is true of the rabbit, but, understandably, students aren't too keen on eating Flopsy. It would, however, take care of the annual "who takes care of the rabbit over the summer" problem.)

Beyond elementary school, teachers can use more than one sieve for presenting the ocean of scientific material. Tending the bean plants and taking care of Flopsy give way to biology, the study of living things—plants (botany), animals (zoology), and humans (anatomy and physiology). The solar system model and rock collecting prepare students for physical science, the study of the non-living aspects of the natural world: astronomy, chemistry, geology, meteorology, and physics.

Science as a subject, however, does not stand alone. Just like the interrelated natural world it observes, science depends on other subjects—most specifically, mathematics. Science depends on mathematics like stories depend on words.

Mathematics in the elementary school is dominated by mastering basic arithmetic, memorizing multiplication tables, and laboring through the steps of long division. Budding mathematicians play Around the World for indoor recess, estimate the number of jellybeans in a jar, and wear erasers to nubs solving problems about Sally's seashells or the coins in Bob's pocket.

Before they realize it, our students are face-to-face with geometric proofs and algebraic logarithms. Some of them, perhaps unknowingly, are preparing for careers in business, technology, architecture, engineering, and accounting; their third grade times tables may be a distant memory, but those math facts shaped how these students will make a living. Others' math skills will help them navigate in the kitchen, putter around the workshop, and persevere through the weeks leading up to April 15 every year. Even in a world of calculators and computers, math skills are an integral aspect of life.

While science and math may favor our more analytical students, a basic understanding of the natural world is a vital part of every student's understanding of who God is and what their place is in His created world.

Introduction

ALTHOUGH THE Bible shapes the way we read and teach science, it is not a science book. Nonetheless, like our students who skip the assigned reading and just hunt for answers to complete their homework, we often come to the Bible looking for answers to our scientific questions, rather than letting the text speak for itself and tell us what is most important. This tendency is perhaps nowhere more evident than in our reading of the Genesis account of creation.

The human author of Genesis, working in tandem with the Divine Author, had an agenda when he wrote the book, but it was not to answer the precise questions of modern science. He was not concerned with the day-age theory, the gap theory, or how light existed before the sun, moon, and stars. His agenda was entirely theological. He intended to communicate important truth about God, evident from his opening statement: "In the beginning, God . . ." God is the first subject of the entire Bible, and He remains its primary subject all the way through Revelation. The author also intended to communicate truths about people as God's creation.

Approaching Genesis on its own terms may not help your students identify rocks or solve quadratic equations, but it will help them understand profound truths about the God who created the rocks and who lies behind the orderly world of mathematics. It will show them who God is: the sovereign creator, a compassionate provider, and an imaginative designer. They will see a God who created the world for the benefit and enjoyment of the people He would put on it. As your students understand who God is through the Genesis account, they will also come to understand their part in His created world: they are created to be dependent creatures, worshipful subjects, and concerned caretakers.

The study of nature *and* the study of Genesis reveal that God is (and has always been) in control. They demonstrate that He created a world for the benefit and enjoyment of people who would care for it and put it to good use, thereby glorifying Him.

Who God Is—Sovereign Creator

> In the beginning, God created the heavens and the earth.
> (Gen 1:1)

Genesis 1:1–2:3 gives the first telling of the creation account. It begins with an amazing cluster of five words: "In the beginning, God created." Stop reading, look out your window, and say it aloud, slowly. In the beginning, God created. Captured in these five deceptively simple words are some of the most profound elements of a Christian worldview. In the beginning, God created.

First, God exists. He makes no attempt to explain or prove His existence. He merely declares it and we are expected to believe it. Whereas the heavens and the earth have an explainable beginning, God does not. He has always been. He is eternal.

If God does not attempt to prove His own existence, perhaps we shouldn't try so hard either. He assumes we will accept His word on the matter. The Bible calls this faith: "By faith we understand that the universe was formed at God's command, so that what is seen was not made out of what was visible . . . And without faith it is impossible to please God, because anyone who comes to him must believe that he exists and that he rewards those who earnestly seek him" (Heb 11:3, 6).

Second, God is the initiator. In the beginning *God* created. This entire cosmological enterprise is *His* story. He began it, and ultimately, He will end it—and He is well in control of everything that happens until then. We are participants in a drama much larger than our own lives: the world is not about us.

When we complete the Bible's first sentence, we gain another foundational truth of the Christian worldview. "In the beginning, God created the heavens and the earth." The verb *created*, used throughout the creation account, is only used in the Bible to describe God's activity. He stands alone as Creator. In this statement, we discover that there are two, and only two, spheres of reality: God and "not-God." Creator and created. In His creative act, God clearly established the boundaries between Himself and everything else.[1] God exists in Himself and everything He created ex-

---

1. One of the many marvels of the incarnation of Jesus Christ is that His presence on earth represents the only time that the line between Creator and creation is bridged—God

ists because He chose to make it. He is the answer to the question, "Where did everything come from?"

Our curiosity may drive us to know *how* it all happened, but God did not think it terribly important that we understand it all—He just wanted us to know that it happened, and that He did it. This is a reality that must be accepted by faith, just as we must accept God's existence by faith.

In this very first statement of the Bible, God confronts us with a critical choice, a life and death choice. He is either God, or He is not. If we acknowledge Him as He has revealed Himself—as the Creator—we can continue reading. If we deny His self-revelation, then we must close the Bible and choose a different explanation for our existence, sustenance, salvation, and eternity. Everything begins in Genesis 1.

Seeing God in Every Day—Compassionate Provider and Imaginative Designer

It has been said that we cannot wake up in the morning without bumping into God. His reflection is everywhere in the world we experience. It is under, above, around, and inside us. Some of it is visible—like the water from your spigot, the strawberries in your breakfast bowl, and the snowflakes on your windshield. Some is invisible—like the air you breathe, the fragrance of blooming lilacs, and warmth of the summer sun. We hear, see, smell, taste, and touch glimpses of God who created everything for the benefit of humankind. He is a compassionate provider. We also catch glimpses of how God created everything for our enjoyment: He is an imaginative designer concerned with detail, beauty, and variety.

The emphasis throughout the remainder of this chapter—a journey through the seven days of creation—is how the natural world reflects God and His care to make a world that could sustain enjoyable human life. As our students begin to understand God, they should be prompted to respond to Him through praise and obedience.

Creation

Day One

> Now the earth was formless and empty, darkness was over the surface of the deep, and the Spirit of God was hovering over the waters.

---

the eternal Son, second person of the Trinity, took on the form of a created being. Jesus was the God-man—and will be both God and man forever.

> And God said, "Let there be light," and there was light. God saw that the light was good, and he separated the light from the darkness. God called the light "day," and the darkness he called "night." And there was evening, and there was morning—the first day. (Gen 1:2–5)

When it was created, the earth was just a giant sphere covered with water and darkness—a place where the Spirit of God hovered. It was empty and formless. Then God moved. By the power of His spoken word, He transformed an empty and formless sphere into a beautiful and magnificent habitat for humans, animals, and plants.

On what would become the first day, His voice thundered into the darkness, "Let there be light!" At His command, the darkness fled and light filled the expanse of the heavens. It wasn't the sun—that doesn't appear until the fourth day—but it *was* light.[2]

Light is something we take for granted until a storm knocks out the power in the middle of the night. Suddenly we are engulfed in darkness. Thick darkness. Our first reaction is to find light; we have to be able to see. So, while trying to avoid stubbing our toes on dresser legs or kitchen chairs, we grope around the house in search of the seldom-used flashlight. When we finally find it, it dispels the darkness in an instant—that is, if the batteries aren't dead.

What exactly is light, this thing created by God that we cannot live without?

The light that illumines our surroundings is called visible light, and while indispensable to our lives, it is only a small part of a much larger picture. When God spoke those first creative words, He created more than light: He called into existence the electromagnetic spectrum, an amazing scientific reality that allows us to hear music on the radio, cook dinner in the microwave, take X rays of broken bones, and even fight cancer . . . all in addition to being able to see things in color.

Light seems so simple. It dispels darkness. It keeps us from things that go bump in the night. Yet, light is so much more than meets the eye. It is a finely tuned coordination between one narrow segment of electromagnetic waves, the communication between our eyes and brains, and our God-endowed ability to correctly understand the natural world in the way He intended. God created light for our benefit—and also for our

---

2. The universe existed with light, but not sunlight, for three days. We have trouble comprehending this since life as we know it is dependent on the light of the sun. However, we only have to read through the rest of the Story to realize that someday we won't need the light of the sun—the world will be fully lighted by the presence of God (Rev 22).

enjoyment. The human capacity for sight is a treasured gift, a gift most of us take for granted.

> God saw that the light was good. (Gen 1:4)

Day Two

> And God said, "Let there be an expanse between the waters to separate water from water." So God made the expanse and separated the water that was under the expanse from the water above it. And it was so. God called the expanse "sky." And there was evening and there was morning—the second day. (Gen 1:6–8)

Water, water, *everywhere*! Water above, water below—everything was water. On the second day of creation, God brought some order to the watery chaos. He made a separation between the water above the earth and the water covering the earth—He created sea and sky, ocean and atmosphere. All the earth was ocean and all the sky was atmosphere—and the firmament separated the two. On this day, God created habitats for what He would create on the fifth day: a sky for the birds and a sea for the fish. In creating the atmosphere, however, He also added a necessary element to *our* habitat: air.

The invisible blanket of air that surrounds the earth is so intertwined with our well-being that we, quite simply, cannot exist without it—yet strangely we are generally unaware of it (unless it is allergy season). Air, a combination of mostly nitrogen and oxygen, weighs heavily on us, but we never even feel it—we just breathe it. Only because of God's incredible design, we are not crushed by the nearly one ton of air pressing down on us (and you thought your book bag was heavy). We can, amazingly, even freely jump and move in this highly "pressurized" atmosphere.

The atmosphere is a vast expanse of activity, in addition to the birds, kites, and planes that all share space in the sky. It is the conduit for weather—clouds, temperature, precipitation, and wind. We are surrounded by the uncontrollable forces of weather, something that is of special concern to us on spring days when we have planned field trips to the zoo or on winter days when we could really use a snow day. At its worst, weather can threaten our property and our lives, but even on average days, it has its effects: it changes our moods, wreaks havoc on our sinuses, and causes indoor recess (thus wreaking havoc on our sanity).

The atmosphere, the earth, and the sun have an interlocking relationship. The earth and its inhabitants depend on this relationship for survival.

We need air for breathing and shade to protect us from the sun, we need precipitation so our gardens grow, we need the sun to heat the earth's surface, and we appreciate winds that warm or cool us in extreme weather.

And we have control over none of it! God is in charge. Some days we want sun for our golf outing, and we want rain for the lawn, but weather is not like a take-out order. God has established the atmosphere with its wind patterns and its zones of hot, temperate, and polar regions—each with consistent patterns of climate. Within these patterns of climate, all weather occurs under the control of the Creator God.

In the book of Job, God reminds Job—and us—that He is in charge of all that happens in the atmosphere:

> Then the Lord answered Job out of the storm. He said, "Who is this that darkens my counsel with words without knowledge? Brace yourself like a man; I will question you, and you shall answer me. Where were you when I laid the earth's foundation? Tell me if you understand. . . . Have you entered the storehouses of the snow or seen the storehouses of the hail? . . . What is the way to the place where the lightning is dispersed, or the place where the east winds are scattered over the earth? . . . Does the rain have a father? Who fathers the drops of dew? . . . Can you raise your voice to the clouds and cover yourself with a flood of water? Do you send the lightning bolts on their way? Do they report to you, 'Here we are'? . . . Who has the wisdom to count the clouds? Who can tip over the water jars of heaven when the dust becomes hard and the clods of earth stick together?" (Job 38)

God did not expect Job to answer. He just needed to remind him that He is in charge. He designed the atmosphere for the welfare of earth's inhabitants—we need air and water to survive. He created it for our enjoyment—does the sky have to be so blue? does lightning have to be so magnificent?

> And it was so. (Gen 1:7b)

Day Three

> And God said, "Let the water under the sky be gathered to one place, and let the dry ground appear." And it was so. God called the dry ground "land," and the gathered waters he called "seas." And God saw that it was good. Then God said, "Let the land produce vegetation: seed-bearing plants and trees on the land that bear fruit with seed in it, according to their various kinds." And it was so.

> The land produced vegetation: plants bearing seed according to their kinds and trees bearing fruit with seed in it according to their kinds. And God saw that it was good. And there was evening, and there was morning—the third day. (Gen 1:9–13)

On day three, God continued making the earth a habitable place for life, especially human life. He gathered the water into oceans and raised up dry land. While we cannot be sure about the topography of this original land since the flood later drastically altered the landscape, we know that ultimately the land became a fascinating mosaic of forms—mountains, valleys, deserts, and forests.

Our globe is adorned with mountains as high as Mount Everest (29,028 feet) and valleys as deep as the Mariana Trench in the Pacific Ocean (36,201 feet)—a difference of 12.35 miles! Deserts, terrain so desolate that few plants and animals can survive in them, are found on all seven continents except Europe, and they cover a fifth of the earth's land surface. Forests blanket another third of the land with sturdy redwoods, fragrant pines, sprawling oaks, swaying palm trees, blossoming apple trees, and approximately 20,000 other kinds of trees that grow in the climates best suited for them.

God also covered much of the land surface with about ten inches of topsoil, the only layer of soil in which plants will grow well and an indispensable part of sustaining human life. We depend on soil to grow plants, and we depend on plants and their provisions like food, shade, wood, and oxygen.

The psalmist in a hymn of praise to God said:

> Praise the LORD, O my soul.
> O LORD my God, you are very great;
>   you are clothed with splendor and majesty . . .
> He waters the mountains from his upper chambers;
>   the earth is satisfied by the fruit of his work.
> He makes grass grow for the cattle,
>   and plants for man to cultivate—
>   bringing forth food from the earth:
> wine that gladdens the heart of man,
>   oil to make his face shine,
>   and bread that sustains his heart. (Ps 104:1, 13–15)

> And God saw that it was good. (Gen 1:10b, 12b)

Nature

Day Four

> And God said, "Let there be lights in the expanse of the sky to separate the day from the night, and let them serve as signs to mark seasons and days and years, and let them be lights in the expanse of the sky to give light on the earth." And it was so. God made two great lights—the greater light to govern the day and the lesser light to govern the night. He also made the stars. God set them in the expanse of the sky to give light on the earth, to govern the day and the night, and to separate light from darkness. And God saw that it was good. And there was evening, and there was morning—the fourth day. (Gen 1:14–19)

On day four of creation, God moved His creative activity into the far reaches of space when He made the sun, moon, and stars. Even there, however, He created things for the benefit of people, contributing to a world in which they could live and a place they could enjoy.

Perfectly positioned in space, the sun provides heat and light essential for our existence. If it were a little closer to the earth, we would burn up; a little farther away, and we would freeze. In the beginning God put it in just the right place for our benefit—and it has stayed there ever since.

The sun, the "greater light to govern the day," comes over the horizon every morning, rain or shine, and goes down over the horizon every evening, without fail. We never have to be concerned about it; our only "concern" is trying to catch the beautiful scenery on a clear night or being up early enough to enjoy the soft start of a new day. Likewise the seasons change without any effort on our part. We plan our lives knowing that the sun will always come up in the morning and summer will always follow spring. God is a God of order, and He put measures of time in the heavens to demonstrate His character every day.

The moon, the "lesser light to govern the night," came up close and personal into our living rooms on the night of July 20, 1969, when Neil Armstrong and Buzz Aldrin stepped from their lunar module, the Eagle, onto the cratered surface of the moon. After watching the historic landing and the astronauts' frolic on the moon, Richard stepped out our backdoor, looked up at the moon shining so brightly, and marveled that God had given humans the ability to understand the workings of space so they could plot a course to the moon more than 200,000 miles away and make a pinpoint landing at a preplanned site after having taken into account the speeding earth and its satellite and earth's and moon's gravity.

This "one small step for man, one giant leap for mankind" was indeed historic, but even at that, we were only walking in God's footprints. More amazing than the lunar landing is the fact that God prescribed constant patterns of movement to the earth and the moon that scientists have uncovered and learned how to use.

Pictures from that remarkable night make it look as if the earth's desolate satellite does not have much value. It has no light of its own and it is uninhabitable. Yet without the reflected light of the moon, night would be coal black. Limited moonlight provides enough illumination to allow people to find their way around after dark. Additionally, its gravitational pull on earth's ocean waters cause the daily rise and fall of the tide.

Stars, probably the least known of the heavenly bodies, are also some of the most fascinating. Their sheer size and incredible distance from earth are beyond our ability to comprehend. Even those in our own Milky Way galaxy are far away. The distance across our galaxy in miles is 586 followed by fifteen zeros. Distances between stars are four to five light years, or 23.4–29.3 trillion miles—that has twelve zeroes behind it. Our own sun, a star, lies about two-thirds of the way out from the center of the Milky Way, and one of its trips around the center of the galaxy takes about 200 million years. Scientists tell us that there are many more galaxies similar to ours. The size of the universe is incomprehensible.

Though their practical usefulness to us may be limited, the starry heavens and the distant galaxies teach us something important about God: He is infinite, vast, and unknowable in so many ways. We know about God to the extent that He has revealed Himself through the natural world and through His written and living Word—and even then, we have so much to learn!—but we can not begin to imagine how much we do not know about Him. He created the uncountable, unreachable stars in distant galaxies for us to enjoy on clear nights, but also to remind us how small and limited we are in comparison to Him. The only appropriate response of human beings to such a God is worship and obedience.

> The heavens declare the glory of God;
> > the skies proclaim the work of his hands.
> Day after day they pour forth speech;
> > night after night they display knowledge.
> There is no speech or language
> > where their voice is not heard.
> Their voice goes out into all the earth,
> > their words to the ends of the world.
> In the heaven he has pitched a tent for the sun,

> which is like a bridegroom coming forth from his pavilion,
> like a champion rejoicing to run his course.
> It rises at one end of the heavens
> and makes its circuit to the other;
> nothing is hidden from its heat. (Ps 19:1–6)
>
> And God saw that it was good. (Gen 1:18b)

Day Five

> And God said, "Let the water teem with living creatures, and let birds fly above the earth across the expanse of the sky." So God created the great creatures of the sea and every living and moving thing with which the water teems, according to their kinds, and every winged bird according to its kind. And God saw that it was good. God blessed them and said, "Be fruitful and increase in number and fill the water in the seas, and let the birds increase on the earth." And there was evening and there was morning—the fifth day. (Gen 1:20–23)

On day five, God turned His attention back to the earth. Having made empty but inhabitable regions on the earth, God set about the task of filling them. He filled the seas with fish and other creatures suitable for them, and He filled the skies with birds. In doing so, He again contributed to the benefit and enjoyment of people.

Oceans, lakes, and streams are treasure troves of useful resources. We need the protein, minerals, fats, and vitamins found in seafood. We use the iodine and algin from seaweed (iodine is in our saltshakers and algin helps hold ice cream, salad dressings, aspirin, and chocolate milk together), we harvest pearls from oysters, and during World War I the plant kelp was even harvested from the sea to make explosives and fertilizers.

But bodies of water and their inhabitants also exist for our enjoyment. An avid fisherman loves nothing more than rising in the morning mist to cast his line into a quiet pool of water. Children cannot find better entertainment on a hot summer day than catching frogs near the water. Scuba divers mingle with aquatic life just for the thrill of its beauty. God has filled the waters of the earth with many wonderful creatures and plants, out of sight under the water, but very much part of our lives.

Having filled the waters of the earth, God then filled the skies—with nearly nine thousand species of birds! The bird collection includes backyard and field birds, water and land birds, game birds, tropical birds,

birds of prey, and perching birds. One of the most awesome sights in the sky is to watch an eagle soar and then swoop down to pick up a "take out" dinner in its powerful talons, or to watch a mother robin carry bits of night crawlers to her nest and drop them into the open beaks of her chirping babies.

We gain many benefits from birds. Not only do we savor the flavor of roasted turkey on Thanksgiving or barbequed wings at a summer picnic, we gain much from many of them *before* we eat them. Some birds eat harmful insects, minimizing damage to farm crops. Others, like hawks and owls, eat small rodents, reducing the loss of valuable grains. Chickens share their eggs with us for breakfast. And others, like parakeets and parrots, can make good pets if you like listening to talking birds.

We marvel at a wide variety of species for their beautiful coloring, predictable flight patterns, ways of eating, and their unique songs or calls. The most fascinating quality about birds is that they show forth the glory of God by following built-in instincts and behavior patterns that have remained unchanged for thousands of years. These by-the-clock patterns assure us that God still sustains the universe.

God said, "Let the birds increase on the earth," and they continue to do so for our benefit and enjoyment.

> And God saw that it was good. (Gen 1:21b)

Day Six: Part One

> And God said, "Let the land produce living creatures according to their kinds; livestock, creatures that move along the ground, and wild animals, each according to its kind." And it was so. God made the wild animals according to their kinds, the livestock according to their kinds, and all the creatures that move along the ground according to their kinds. And God saw that it was good. (Gen 1:24–25)
>
> Now the Lord God had formed out of the ground all the beasts of the field and all the birds of the air. He brought them to the man to see what he would name them; and whatever the man called each living creature, that was it name. So the man gave names to all the livestock, the birds of the air and all the beasts of the field. (Gen 2:19–20)

On the sixth day, God made land creatures—an astronomical number of species. We will reference only a sampling of groups that provide benefits for us and affect the way we live our lives: domesticated animals, wild animals, and insects.

Domesticated animals include everything from cows to horses to house pets. Many of these animals—cattle, sheep, and hogs—are raised for their meat, a major staple of diets worldwide. Milk is another major animal product obtained from domesticated animals. These kinds of animals have served humans very well as "beasts of burden." From ancient times horses, camels, donkeys, mules, and oxen have helped people by breaking up the soil for planting, pulling wagons and carriages from place to place, and carrying goods and people on their backs across deserts, country roads, and city streets.

Another domesticated group of animals is pets, those creatures we select as companions. Almost any animal can become a pet, but the most popular are dogs, cats, birds, and fish. People in different cultures train some exotic animals as pets, such as monkeys, snakes, mongooses, and kangaroos. Keeping pets is a universal activity and provides many people with loyal, obedient, and fun companions.

God's generous provision of a variety of domesticated animals has provided dietary necessities, livelihoods, and pleasures for people in every part of the world.

A second group of animals that impact our lives are those we fear, the "wild animals." They are considered wild because they resist human intrusions and attempts to domesticate or control them. Most are hardy and wily and prolific procreators, and they are elusive and frustrating to control.[3] Some we fear at a distance—those from far away places like jungles, polar regions, and deserts that we typically only see in the zoo, such as lions, tigers, bears, snakes, alligators, and porcupines. Others that we fear live in our neighborhoods, backyards, and maybe even in our homes—rodents, bats, spiders, and wasps. These creatures are found everywhere, and they are able to take care of themselves, living out their life cycles without any help from humans.

Finally, God created the tiniest land creatures: insects—more than 800,000 kinds! How many is that? World Book encyclopedia once figured that if the scientific names of every kind of insects were printed in *World Book*, it would take more than 6,000 pages to list them.[4] That's a lot of

---

3. Interestingly, these animals were not created to be feared. In the original, sinless creation, all creatures were herbivores and none were threatened by others. It was only after the fall that animal groups became wild and dangerous. And it was not until much later, after the great flood, that God told people they could eat the meat of animals (Gen 9:3).

4. Watt, "Insects," 278.

bugs! If that is not enough to make your skin crawl, scientists discover thousands of new species every year.

While many insects, like flies and mosquitoes, are rarely anything but annoying, other insects help us by pollinating plants, providing food for birds and other animals, making honey, and eating other insects.

> And God saw that it was good.
> (Gen 1:25b)

Day Six: Part Two

> Then God said, "Let us make man in our image, in our likeness, and let them rule over the fish of the sea and the birds of the air, over the livestock, over all the earth, and over all the creatures that move along the ground." So God created man in his own image, in the image of God created he him; male and female he created them. (Gen 1:26–27)

> The Lord God formed the man from the dust of the ground and breathed into his nostrils the breath of life, and the man became a living being. (Gen 2:7)

We are finally ready for the culminating event of God's creative activities—human beings, male and female created in God's image and likeness. During the second part of the sixth day, God created the man from the ground and breathed into him "the breath of life." Later, He created the woman from a rib removed from the man's side.

People have a lot in common with the animals that God created earlier. He used the same creative pattern for the man and the woman that He used for the other creatures, and He breathed into them the same breath of life. He made the human body with the same systems as many other creatures, including respiratory, circulatory, digestive, reproductive, skeletal, muscular, and nervous. The people, the creatures, and even the plants need what God made on the first four days: they all function interdependently with sunlight, air, water, land, seasons, days and nights, and years.

If man and animals have so much in common, why don't we believe, like the evolutionists, that people evolved from the animals and merely represent a higher form of life? Most obviously, we do not believe it because that is not how Genesis describes it as happening. Not only did people not evolve from animals but God did something unique in their creation. He made man and woman different than anything else He made. The difference is that humans were created in the image of God—the only element in all of God's creative activity of which this can be said. We will discuss this concept extensively in the next chapter, but part of it includes the responsibility to take care of the earth and its creatures. Although they have much in common with the rest of creation, people were created with an entirely different function than the rest of the living creatures.

As we pause to reflect on these first six days of creation, we have to echo the words of Paul Davies, a professor of mathematical physics:

> Human beings have always been awe struck by the subtlety, majesty, and intricate organization of the physical world. The march of the heavenly bodies across the sky, the rhythms of the seasons, the pattern of a snowflake, the myriads of living creatures so well adapted to their environments—all these things seem too well arranged to be a mindless accident.[5]

Even though Davies is committed to discovering the scientific secrets of the universe apart from God's involvement, he cannot help but acknowledge the order, complexity, and finely tuned functioning of the many systems, creatures, and plants in the universe and on the earth. He recognizes that all of creation, the near and the far, the visible and the invisible, the minute and the huge, all proclaim order in their composition and in their function. How much more should we, those who believe in a sovereign Creator who carefully designed a beautiful and functional world for His own glory—and our benefit and enjoyment—marvel at the God we discover through the study of science and math.

> God saw all that he had made, and it was very good. (Gen 1:31a)

Day Seven

> Thus the heavens and earth were completed in all their vast array. By the seventh day God had finished the work he had been doing; so on the seventh day he rested from all his work. And God blessed the seventh day and made it holy, because on it he rested from all the work of creating that he had done. (Gen 2:1–4)

God's creative activity did not officially end on the sixth day. Genesis records the seventh day, a day that becomes a pervading theme through all of Scripture. For six days, God had been actively bringing the natural world into existence. His work was now completed, and on the seventh day He rested. He stopped working and set apart the seventh day as holy.

---

5. Davies, *The Mind of God*, 194.

God set it apart to be a day for us to refocus our lives on what is central. God created us as creatures that depend on Him for life and everything necessary for it and who also need to stop the normal activities of work and remember Him. He is God; He has made the earth and filled it with plants and animals and beauty and made us like Himself.

Our lives become very busy, and in this busyness God can easily be pushed to the periphery of our lives. God understands this and therefore in the very beginning He set a pattern of rest for our benefit and His glory. On one day in seven, He calls us to pull Him in from the periphery and reorder our lives, making Him the center of our attention. James Grier says it best:

> On Sabbath conditioned by creation, on a regular basis, we come back to acknowledge that we are creatures, that there is someone that transcends us who is our creator to whom we owe our loyalty and allegiance, our service and our stewardship, our minds and our wills and our muscles and all of the activities that we perform in the other six days. It is only because of him that I have capacity and ability to do any of it.[6]

We have been busy in these pages comprehending the natural world that God has made. In the spirit of Sabbath, let us pause and offer our praise to God using Psalm 148 as our hymn of praise:

> Praise the LORD.
> Praise the LORD from the heavens,
>   praise him in the heights above.
> Praise him, all his angels,
>   praise him, all his heavenly hosts.
> Praise him, sun and moon,
>   praise him, all you shining stars.
> Praise him, you highest heavens,
>   and you waters above the skies.
> Let them praise the name of the LORD,
>   for he commanded and they were created.
> He set them in place forever and ever;
>   he gave a decree that will never pass away.
> Praise the LORD from the earth,
>   you great sea creatures and all ocean depths,
>   lightning and hail, snow and clouds,
>   stormy winds that do his bidding,
>   you mountains and all hills,

---

6. Grier, *The Ten Words*, audiotape of lecture 5.

> fruit trees and all cedars,
>   wild animals and all cattle,
> small creatures and flying birds,
> kings of the earth and all nations
>   you princes and all rulers on earth,
> young men and maidens,
>   old men and children.
> Let them praise the name of the LORD,
>   for his name alone is exalted;
>   his splendor is above the earth and the heavens.
> He has raised up for his people a horn,
>   the praise of all his saints,
>   of Israel, the people close to his heart.
> Praise the LORD. (Ps 148)

Then and Now

> God saw all that he had made, and it was very good. (Gen 1:31a)

This closing statement is God's assessment of the world He had created, the world that the man and the woman were to rule over. Every part of this amazing creation is dependent on other parts of the natural world, and ultimately, all are dependent on God.

But part of helping our students understand the world God has made includes helping them realize that the way things are on earth now is not what has always been, nor what will always be. The earth has undergone significant changes since God's creative beginning. Any study of the natural world from within a Christian worldview requires that we recognize two things at the outset: (1) God made it; (2) man damaged it.

The way the world works changed following the sin of Adam and Eve who were living in a perfect environment. Their rebellion against God in the garden resulted in death—to them and to their surroundings. God placed a curse on the very ground He used to create Adam. From that moment on, the soil—home of the plant kingdom—produced weeds that severely complicated the efforts of Adam and his descendants to grow food. Human beings would have to toil and sweat as they cultivated the soil and continually competed with the weeds for mastery (Gen 3:1–24).

In our study of the natural world, we must help our students understand that the laws of nature, contrary to what science teaches us, are not "constant" in the sense that they have always been and will always be the same. For example, scientists know that every living thing is in the process of dying. No matter how scientifically savvy we become, we are unable to reverse this "law of nature." However, this is neither the way things were before sin entered the world, nor the way they will be on the new earth when sin is gone forever. The "law" will change. Also, animals that we know as carnivores have not always been that way—as previously mentioned, the creation account makes it clear that all living creatures ate only green plants, not each other. Furthermore, there is coming a new day when the lion will lay with the lamb, not tear it to shreds for dinner.

Nature and School Subjects

Whether or not our students have the curiosity, aptitude, and perseverance it takes for a career in science or mathematics, none of them should engage in study of the natural world and its governing principles without acquiring a deeper understanding of the Creator. Every page in every science and math book, regardless of the worldview behind them, shows Him to be a sovereign creator, a compassionate provider, and an imaginative designer. We dare not let our students miss it. We also dare not let them miss the role they play in His creation—as dependent creatures, worshipful subjects, and concerned caretakers.

Science—"The Other Book"

Science is the study of what theologians call general revelation—what we learn about God from what He has revealed in creation. Contemporary culture has drawn a sharp dividing line between faith and science, and most people (including many Christians) have bought into this division. But in reality, we ought to hold the Bible in one hand and a science book in the other: both inform us about God, and there is complete agreement (hard-won sometimes) between the two. One of the most important things a Christian science teacher can do is to teach students to think critically (and "Christianly") about theories and to read the Bible carefully.

Health and Physical Education—Making It Personal

Science becomes personal in health class. Health professionals are increasingly aware that non-physical factors affect our well-being, and more and more clinics are including "spirituality" in their wellness programs. We all know that there is more to health than blood and tissue, but why? The naturalist worldview does not allow for this, although most of its adherents will not admit that in naturalism the human body is reduced to a machine. Only the Christian worldview explains the full-orbed people we know ourselves to be. Teaching students *all* aspects of health and how to care for their bodies (gifts from God!) is the focus of Christian teaching in these subjects.

Mathematics—the Expression of Order

Math is a subject that seems to serve as a dividing line between students: they either love it or they hate it. They either "get it" or they don't. And more than any other subject, it seems to cause great angst and anxiety for those who don't. Ironically, the discipline that exhibits God's orderliness more than any other discipline is lost in a jumble of numbers and rules that don't make sense in the Math Hater's head. While we search for ways to clear the blockage and help our less logically minded students understand how math works, we need to keep before them the bigger picture of God. Math fits within the revelation of God, but God is also big enough to have many, many aspects that we do not fully understand.

Summary of Truths

In this chapter we have discussed significant truths we learn from the account of creation about God and His existence, as well as how we see His power, goodness, glory, intellect, and order in the created order.

The Person of God

1. God is. He does not attempt to prove His existence, but merely declares it. Therefore we do not attempt to prove it; we accept His word regarding it.
2. God is the initiator. He is the first subject in the Bible, and the entire Book is about Him. Everything we study outside the Bible is also part of His Story.
3. God is eternal. He had no beginning and He has no end.
4. God is separate and distinct from what He created. There are two spheres of reality—God and "created-by-God."
5. God created everything. Everything but God had a beginning.
6. God alone is worthy of worship and obedience.

God in the Created Order

1. God displays His power in the natural world through an endless array.
    a. The ability to bring into existence the massive great blue whale as well as the microscopic human cell containing volumes of information.
    b. The ability to form majestic mountain ranges with snow-covered peaks.
    c. The ability to create towering redwood trees and the lily of the valley with its simplicity and lovely fragrance.
    d. The ability to call into existence much of the natural world by the power of His word.

2. God displays His goodness in the natural world in many ways.
    a. The variety and abundance of plants for food for all people—both God lovers and God haters.
    b. The creation of creatures for food, for beasts of burden, and for family pets.
    c. The beauty of flowering plants for gardeners to nurture and enjoy.
    d. The provision of rain to water the ground and aid in plant growth.

3. God displays His glory through all the created elements.
    a. We stand in awe of the natural world in its complexities and its variety.
    b. His works are beyond our power to duplicate or improve upon.
    c. God declared the natural world to be "good" and "very good" because it reflects His glory in a most magnificent way.
    d. We lack the language to describe the wonders and our amazement and awe. The only response is to be thankful that we have been granted the privilege of experiencing God's wonderful universe and voicing to Him in word, song, or dance our deeply felt gratitude.

4. God reveals something of His great intellect.
    a. He created each plant and creature with its built-in life cycle and gave most the ability to live without human help.
    b. Millions of people have been working for thousands of years to uncover and learn the secrets of the natural world and still we do not know where the end is.

Nature

    c. The earth and the universe are complex integrated systems that require all of their components working together to maintain life.
5. God is a God of order, evident in many facets of the created world.
    a. Every heavenly body follows its orbit through space, each orbit organized in such a way as to prevent bodies from colliding with each other.
    b. Each group of animals and its members maintain their distinctiveness through the structure imposed by God—they reproduce after their own kind.
    c. Each species has its unique food menu so there is enough to go around for all species.
6. God has revealed much about Himself through the natural world so that people are without excuse regarding His existence and person:

> The wrath of God is being revealed from heaven against the godlessness and wickedness of men who suppress the truth by their wickedness, since what may be known about God is plain to them. For since the creation of the world God's invisible qualities—his eternal power and divine nature—have been clearly seen, being understood from what has been made, so that men are without excuse. (Rom 1:18–20)

7. God, an infinite being, created an infinite universe. When finite human beings use only their finite intellects and resources in a fallen world to understand/explain the infinite universe apart from a transcendent Creator, they glorify themselves . . . not the Creator.

Teaching Tips

1. The Gift (and the Power) of Sight. Help your students better appreciate the gift of sight by blindfolding them for part of the day, or, if you are unprepared to handle a classroom of "blind" students, have them do a blindfolded evening or weekend at home. When they have completed the exercise, have them write down their thoughts about the experience and talk about them in class. Read excerpts from Helen Keller's writing or a story about her. Include a discussion of how "sight" and "eyes" are used in the Bible. For younger students, you can do this by looking at the stories of blind people (being healed); those led astray by temptation through the eyes (e.g., Eve, Samson); psalms that talk about seeing God's works; proverbs that address "sight" or

"eyes." For older students, build off these stories: have them do a topical study of "eyes" and "sight" in Scripture; develop the idea of eyes as windows that require careful guarding (i.e., what we see is indelibly impressed on our minds); discuss how "sight" can lead to sin; you can even incorporate ideas of world"view" with your older students. (All grade levels, with variation)

2. To Near Infinity . . . and Beyond! Talking about the vastness of the solar system is one thing, but walking it is quite another. Gather the following supplies: yellow recess ball (or similar), a poppy seed, a BB, a pea, a pin, a ping-pong ball, and a big marble. Take your students outside and leave a couple of them with the yellow recess ball at your starting point. This is a severely undersized sun. Start walking, counting steps in a close-to-scale reconstruction of the solar system. After thirty-five steps (each step is a million miles), leave a few more students with the poppy seed for Mercury; thirty more steps and a BB for Venus; twenty-eight more steps and the pea for the cosmic position of Earth. At this point, you may want to call in your stranded students so they don't miss out on traveling into deep space (and since it is unwise to leave students standing alone on city sidewalks). Go forty-four more steps and set some students with a pinhead for Mars; three hundred thirty steps and a ping-pong ball for Jupiter; three hundred eighty-three steps and a marble for Saturn. At this point (if you haven't already run out of space), it's time to imagine. Walking another mile and a half will get you past Uranus and Neptune, and on your way to Pluto. Thankfully, since Pluto has been demoted from its status as a planet, you don't have to worry about finishing the trip. You almost don't need to do any more talking after this exercise; your students will be dumbfounded. But, take the opportunity anyway to talk about the vastness of God. Ponder passages that echo His greatness: Isaiah 40:12–31; Job 38–41; Psalm 19; Psalm 104. And then also reflect on passages that affirm His detailed interest in our lives: Psalm 16; Psalm 18; Matthew 6:25–34; Philippians 4:6–7; 1 Peter 5:7. (Elementary grades; note that there are many variations of this exercise available online through sites that specialize in teaching astronomy to kids.)

3. Whose View? Bring in a science article from a current non-Christian publication. Read excerpts aloud (or distribute copies) and discuss with your students what the operating worldview is, namely, how does the author view God? How does the author view humans? What

is the author's view of the role of humans? "Rewrite" the article from a theistic point of view: how would the argument be shaped differently? Then have students find their own article and work through the same process, either individually or as a group. Discuss together how we can still learn valuable things from non-Christian worldviews (all truth is God's truth), as long as we recognize the points at which scientists are explaining things from within a closed system. (Junior high and high school)

4. Who's the Boss? Use your playground as a place to harpoon whales (and talk about the environmental concerns associated with this!). Divide into small groups and give each group a clipboard, paper, whale measurements, and sidewalk chalk. (Use your science book or another resource to determine which whales you want and what their measurements are.) Have each group measure and mark the lengths of the specified whales; have them give the whales body shapes, too. After your science discussion of the whales' features, assemble the entire class inside one of the larger whales and review (or tell) the story of Jonah. (Note that the Bible does not say "whale," but "great fish," and we do not know what fish it was. The whales you have drawn are probably not native to the Mediterranean Sea.) Make special note of the fact that God controls the movement of the fish; it becomes God's tool, and a far more "obedient" tool than God's prophet! This is a wonderful lesson for talking about choices; the irony in the storytelling of Jonah is unbeatable: the pagan sailors are more pious than God's prophet; the fish is more obedient than God's prophet; the sinful city is more repentant than God's prophet. (Elementary grades)

5. Standing on Their Shoulders. Each generation adds to the learning of previous generations (we "stand on their shoulders"), and it is important for our students to appreciate the history that leads to present-day disciplines. Compile a list of Christians who have worked in your subject area, and as part of your semester's assigned workload, have students read a biography of a Christian in your field and report in writing or to the class what the person accomplished, how faith influenced his or her studies, and what legacy he or she has left. (Junior high and high school)

Additional Resources[7]

1. DeWitt, Calvin B. *The Environment and the Christian: What Does the Old Testament Say about the Environment?* and *The Environment and the Christian: What Does the New Testament Say about the Environment?* Grand Rapids: Baker Books, 1991. DeWitt is associated with the Au Sable Institute of Environmental Studies (www.ausable.org) and addresses what Christian environmentalists believe to be major problems with today's environment as well as how Christians can be good stewards of the earth. He has several books, many out of print but still available through online sources (including the site for the Au Sable Institute listed above).

2. Hearn, Walter. *Being a Christian in Science.* Downers Grove, IL: InterVarsity Press, 1997. Hearn is a biochemist who encourages Christians to recognize careers in science as calls to ministry. His experience in the field and in the classroom has given him a first-hand perspective on the ethical and professional, as well as spiritual, implications of following a divine calling into science.

3. Martin, Jobe. *Incredible Creatures That Defy Evolution.* 3 volumes. DVD, VHS. Monument, CO: Reel Productions, 2006. A popular series, these videos introduce the complexity of certain creatures with an eye to Intelligent Design. Available through www.explorationfilms.com (or other online sources).

4. Meyer, Stephen C., and W. Peter Allen. *Unlocking the Mystery of Life.* DVD, VHS. La Habra, CA: Illustra Media, 2004. Distributed through The Discovery Institute (see number 8 below), this documentary presents the growing number of scientific challenges to evolution. Available through www.discovery.org (and other online sources).

5. Moreland, J. P. *Scaling the Secular City: A Defense of Christianity.* Grand Rapids: Baker Books, 1987. Apologetic in its scope, this book by philosopher and professor J. P. Moreland especially addresses the philosophy of science.

6. Pearcey, Nancy R., and Charles B. Thaxton, *The Soul of Science: Christian Faith and Natural Philosophy.* Wheaton, IL: Crossway Books, 1994. Science writers Pearcey and Thaxton argue that modern science in the West actually developed *because* of Christianity's belief in an ordered universe. They offer a clear presentation about the "conflict" between religion and science.

---

[7]. Thanks to Dave Conrads and Ray Gates for their help compiling this list of resources.

7. Sanera, Michael, and Jane S. Shaw. *Facts, Not Fear: Teaching Children About the Environment.* 2d ed. Washington, D.C.: Regnery Publishing, 1999. In opposition to DeWitt and the Au Sable Institute's view that there are major environmental problems in the world today, Sanera and Shaw believe the issues are overstated. They set out to give a balanced view of environmental "hot topics."

8. Wells, Jonathan. *Icons of Evolution.* DVD. Palmer Lake, CO: Coldwater Media, 2004. This documentary, based on Wells's book below, is distributed through The Discovery Institute (Seattle). Not a Christian organization, the institute nonetheless has some fine materials that can be thought-provoking and helpful. Available through www.discovery.org (and other online sources).

9. Wells, Jonathan. *Icons of Evolution: Science or Myth? Why Much of What We Teach about Evolution Is Wrong.* Washington, D.C.: Regnery, 2000. Wells does not write as a creationist, but his debunking of evolutionary theory as traditionally taught can provide Christians with a fuller view of the debate in science today. See number 8 above for the documentary based on this book.

10. Wilkinson, Loren, ed. *Earthkeeping in the Nineties: Stewardship of Creation.* Revised ed. Grand Rapids: Eerdmans, 1991. While outdated in terms of the calendar, this book still offers excellent principles of stewardship for today. Wilkinson writes in the same vein as DeWitt above (who contributes to this volume). The book is available through the Au Sable Institute (www.ausable.org) or other online sources.

11. Other organizations whose materials might prove helpful in certain areas include the Creation Research Society (www.creationresearch.org) and Answers in Genesis (www.answersingenesis.org).

2

People

Most of Wendy's memories of elementary school social studies come from fourth and fifth grades when her teacher used the social studies books as means to increase reading skills. The students independently pored over chapters, laboriously identified main ideas and constructed outlines, defined key vocabulary, and answered what seemed to be obscure questions from the end of each chapter.

Wendy does not fault her teacher for using the books this way. Textbooks across the curriculum are important tools for practicing reading skills, especially at the elementary level. In fact, this particular teacher did more to develop Wendy's outlining and note taking skills than anybody else—a well-worn skill she is thankful to have acquired early in life. Nonetheless, the fact that these are her primary memories of "social studies" causes us to think that during elementary school she missed the heart of social studies—the study of society or social relationships, or most basically, the study of people.

Elementary students usually think of subjects like history and geography as the study of facts. They memorize facts about states and capitals, facts about presidents, facts about famous people, facts about important dates—but fail to understand how such facts could possibly matter. In later years when they study government, economics, and sociology, students still often miss the significance of the subject matter. They do not understand that social studies represent the collective memory of humankind, and they do not understand the significance of memory.

Memories make up our identity. The great tragedy of Alzheimer's and other diseases of dementia is that they rob people of memories—and in so doing these diseases steal the identities of people with rich histories. A husband who no longer knows his wife, a mother who does not know her children, and a grandparent who does not recognize grandchildren wear their familial labels with empty eyes because they have lost their connection to a lifetime of experiences. Without memories, they are rootless and alone, adrift on a sea of unrelated circumstances and events.

What is true for individuals is also true for societies and ultimately for the entire human society. Without memories—our history—we will be rootless and alone, disconnected from the life experiences that shaped who

People

we have become as communities, cultures, nations, and a human race. These past events comprise social studies, and without them, our identity is limited at best, and lost at worst.

Sadly, we live in a culture suffering from a form of dementia. Even more sadly, this dementia is largely voluntary. Most people are unconcerned about the collective memory of humankind. Like our young students, they also do not understand that history is the key to understanding present situations and navigating through the mire of future circumstances. They do not recognize that where we have come from can—and should—affect where we go.

Our students need to engage the study of people—what it means to be created in the image of God, what relationships God established for humankind, and how we live responsibly as members of societies and the world. They cannot know their places in God's world until they have acquired the memories that shape their identities—as people, citizens, children, husbands, wives, and friends. Social studies provide them with the opportunity to take their places responsibly in the human race.

Introduction

> Then God said, "Let us make man in our image, in our likeness, and let them rule over the fish of the sea and the birds of the air, over the livestock, over all the earth, and over all the creatures that move along the ground." So God created man in his own image, in the image of God he created him; male and female he created them. God blessed them and said to them, "Be fruitful and increase in numbers; fill the earth and subdue it. Rule over the fish of the sea and the birds of the air and over every living creature that moves on the ground." (Gen 1:26–28)

THE HUMAN race began with one man and one woman in a lush Mesopotamian garden. Today the world has more than six billion inhabitants living in more than 237 nations and territories on six continents.[1] Thanks to the builders of the tower of Babel,[2] these six billion plus

---

1. Johnstone and Mandryk, *Operation World*, 1.

2. Genesis 11:1–9 records that the people living in the early history of humankind decided to build a tower to make a name for themselves. Besides the sins of pride and arrogance, their major sin was an intentional act of disobedience against God's command to fill the earth (Gen 1:28). Instead they planned to stay together using their common language and not scatter over the face of the earth.

God, aware of their plans, confused their language into many languages and sent them packing "over the face of the whole earth" (11:9). Thus began the development of thousands of people groups, each with its unique culture of language, tradition, and religion.

people comprise twelve thousand ethnolinguistic groups, groups of people distinguished by their "self-identity with traditions of common descent, history, customs, and language."[3]

Being one person on a planet of six billion can understandably make us feel a bit insignificant. Even if we have large families and many friends and acquaintances, our spheres of world influence are limited. Most of us will barely make the newspapers, except for a birth announcement and an obituary. In the global scheme of things, we each live in relative obscurity.

Depressing? Lots of people think so, and it's not hard to understand why, especially in a culture that views humans as simply a higher form of primate. A sense of personal significance is hard enough to come by given the size of the world's population, but its difficulty is only amplified by the naturalism that dominates most worldviews.

The Christian worldview dares to ascribe value—and immeasurable value at that—to each human being, no matter how young and unformed or old and weak. The microscopic embryo is a person with intrinsic value. The bedridden octogenarian who cannot put two thoughts together is a person of inestimable worth.

But why? Quite simply, people of all ages, shapes, and sizes are valuable because God values them. The sovereign Creator of the universe crowned human beings with value and dignity by creating them—by creating us—in His image. His unique image stamped on our beings makes us more valuable than anything in all of His amazing creation. He made us persons like Himself in some way, equipping us to relate to Him and to each other and endowing us with unique responsibilities.

What does it mean to bear God's image? In this section, we will discuss some aspects of being image-bearers and how this sets us apart from the rest of creation. We will then look at the relationships and responsibilities God has ordained for human beings and how we are to function in them. Finally, we will explore how image and relationships relate to school subjects. In doing so, we will answer the question, How do we teach our students to live responsibly?

The account of Noah's sons, Shem, Ham and Japheth, in Genesis 10 is the record of the dispersion of the people from Babel.

3. Johnstone and Mandryk, *Operation World*, 756.

Made in His Image

Long before it actually states that God created man and woman in His image, the account of creation emphasizes the fact that human beings are special. First, God spends a rapidly successive five and a half days designing an environment for what He would ultimately create on the final day. When the "big moment" arrives, the action slows dramatically and Genesis records what looks like a frame-by-frame sequence of events. God had saved the best for last. Secondly, the creation of man was preceded by a divine deliberation. Genesis records a conversation God had with Himself: "Let us make man in our image, in our likeness" (Gen 1:26).[4] There was something unique and special about what God was getting ready to do. Finally, God changed His pattern when He created man and woman. He did not speak Adam into existence but formed him from the dust of the earth, and He made Adam's counterpart in an entirely different way—from the rib of the man. From the very beginning, man and woman were special.

This specialness is reinforced by the statement that man and woman were made in God's likeness. Simply stated, this means that God made us like Himself but in very limited ways. He, of course, is eternal, but we are creatures of time. He is infinite, but we are finite. He is all-knowing, all-powerful and sovereign, while we have little bits of knowledge, power, and autonomy. Since God is a spirit, we obviously do not *look* like Him, but His image is reflected in the non-material aspects of who we are. Although sin has distorted and perverted His image in us, it has not destroyed it; we are image-bearers no matter how little our words and actions reflect Him.[5]

The word *image* may bring to mind pictures of idols of wood, stone, or metal, in human and animal likenesses. Many religions claim and worship such objects as their gods. The unseen, eternal God, however, cannot be reduced to such objects. In fact, He repeatedly forbade His people to make Him into some kind of "graven image" to worship. Yet, since the beginning of time, He has been creating representations—images—of Himself in *people*, billions of them, each uniquely patterned after Him.[6]

---

4. This is not a text to prove the existence of the Trinity. It does, however, make room for later revelation as God progressively introduces Himself throughout Scripture as Father, as Son, and as Holy Spirit.

5. One of the most helpful works in this area is *Created in God's Image* by Anthony Hoekema. See the bibliography for a full listing. Many of our thoughts in this section are shaped by his book.

6. Ironically, people have turned these God-created images into objects of worship—there is nothing people love more than themselves. We worship ourselves.

Exactly how we are patterned after Him is a source of continual debate among biblical scholars and theologians. We do not expect to resolve the issue here, but want to provide you with what we believe to be some of the key concepts involved in bearing the image of the eternal God: community, responsibility, and accountability.

Community—Created for Relationship

At the heart of what it means to image God is the idea of community. God is an eternal community of three—Father, Son, and Holy Spirit. The very essence of His person is relationship. When God created "man" in His image, male and female, He made relationships the essence of their existence.

First, they had a relationship with Him (without the "real thing," the image is meaningless), but humanity's relationship with God began—and temporarily ended—in the garden of Eden. God walked and talked with Adam and Eve in perfect fellowship until they disobeyed Him, severing their relationship with Him. He could have cast them out of His presence forever, but instead He began the long journey to the cross to restore intimacy between God and people. Along the way He provided temporary ways for people to be close to Him—offerings and sacrifices.[7]

He also continued to reveal Himself in mighty acts of deliverance and in written words that we now know as Scripture. People who wanted to be close to God obeyed His instructions and communicated with Him through prayer and meditation. After the cross sacrifices are no longer necessary to remove the barrier of sin—Jesus paid it all—but we still fellowship with God through Scripture reading and meditation, prayer, singing, and praising Him for the beauty and endless array of natural treasures. As the image-bearers of God, we are unique in our ability to be in relationship with God and to communicate with Him.

But we are also unique in the depth of our ability to communicate and be in relationship with others of our species. Every member of the human race is connected to Adam—we all, including Eve, came from him, so we are inextricably bound to each other in relationships that should, according to Jesus, be characterized by love (Matt 22:37–40). Just as God loves us, we love others. Just as He responds to us, we respond to others. Because He has graciously provided for our needs, in like manner, we reflect Him by generously providing for others in times of need.

---

7. See the book of Leviticus for extensive details on the sacrificial system of the Old Testament.

In addition to the relationship we have with every member of the human race, God also created us for great intimacy; Adam and Eve were brought together in a relationship of oneness. This most intimate relationship is the one that most closely resembles the Trinity: just as the Trinity is three distinct people characterized by oneness, so husband and wife are two distinct people who live in a relationship characterized by oneness.[8] Other human relationships develop from this primary one to include children and a myriad of other "communities" important to individual growth, maturity, and wellbeing. We will discuss these relationships in greater detail later in this chapter.

Responsibility—Created for Dominion

A second key idea behind what it means to image God is that we stand in His place in the world. We represent Him on this planet in a way similar to that of a foreign ambassador, carrying out the intentions of the one we represent. He made these intentions clear to Adam and Eve when He gave them the responsibility to be fruitful, multiply, and fill the earth. Then He told them to develop the earth's resources, to take what He had made and make it better. Theologian Michael Wittmer explains how this happens:

> I'm always a bit surprised that God didn't take the safe route, content to merely warn Adam and Eve not to mess things up. He could've said something like this: "Children, here's a wonderful world for you to enjoy. Have all the fun you want, just don't break anything."
>
> But he didn't . . . [he] told them to go change things. But how could they improve an already glorious world? By developing it in a distinctively human fashion: Plant the geraniums over there, learn what grows best where and what they most enjoy eating. God wanted Adam and Eve to participate in his ongoing work of creation, to take the raw materials of a perfect world and arrange them to produce the highest possible benefit.[9]

God created the world with everything we need and then commissioned us to put a uniquely human stamp on it. He put us in charge of caring for the earth's inhabitants and developing its natural resources—what an amazing task! Discovering and developing the secrets of the physical world

---

8. The essence of these relationships is different since God is entirely "other" than we are. But as image-bearers, marriage is the closest we can come to understanding the unity and diversity of God.

9. Wittmer, *Heaven Is a Place on Earth*, 124–25.

for the betterment of the entire planet has kept us busy for thousands of years, and still we are continually learning how much we do not know about the world.

This task would be impossible apart from the ways God uniquely equipped people to think and reason, to distinguish between right and wrong, to appreciate beauty, and to make choices. God made us rational, moral beings with freedom to choose.

Rationality

Philosopher René Descartes boiled human existence down to one statement: "I think, therefore I am." We won't get into how he arrived at this conclusion or what exactly he meant by it, but we suggest that our rational ability is more than the sine quo non of human existence: it is a powerful component of our identity as God's image bearers.[10]

The mind is an amazingly complex immaterial part of us. We use it to create thoughts, words, and concepts—in many different areas all at the same time. How is it that we can drive in afternoon traffic, listen to the top-of-the-hour news, and contemplate the agenda for an upcoming meeting all at the same time? How are we able to carry on a conversation with one person while observing the actions of another through our peripheral vision? How is it possible to doze off in a college class but still be tuned in enough to isolate important information for note taking?

Without ever speaking a word, we can use our minds to evaluate issues and reach tentative solutions. We soar into fantasy worlds where things are what we want them to be, and we plunge into the depths of despair where everything is dark and foreboding. With our minds, we engage other people by sharing our thoughts and discovering theirs, and with our minds, we are able to study and understand the world around us in every discipline of study.

Perhaps even more astounding than the complexity of the mind is that each person's mind is different from everyone else's—this is complexity magnified beyond imagination! We are all "wired" a little bit differently. Our world reflects this diversity—we are professors, surgeons, mechanics, air traffic controllers, engineers, secretaries, landscapers, politicians, turf grass specialists, driver's education teachers, and bank tellers. God

---

10. The idea that rational ability is a component of image-bearers does not imply that the one whose rational ability is limited by genetics, disease, or accident is less human than anybody else. The image of God is part of every human being, but because of the fall, His image is marred by sickness and disease—often of the mind. This does not lessen one's humanity or value; it just lessens one's ability to function in the fullness God originally intended.

equipped the world with a diversity of thinkers in order to accomplish all aspects of developing and bettering His world.

Morality

Medieval theologian Anselm of Canterbury said that God is the greatest possible good. Because we each bear the image of the all-good God, we have an innate sense of His goodness and therefore an awareness of what is *not* good—or what is evil.[11] Even very corrupt people who commit grievous crimes have some awareness of the evil of their actions.[12]

We are not suggesting that people are good by nature, nor that any of us can measure up to God's standard of goodness. *Knowing* what is good and *doing* it are two vastly different things. We are depraved people in need of God's saving grace through Jesus Christ. Morality in the fullness of what God intends is not possible apart from this saving grace and separate from His special revelation in Scripture. Nonetheless, even unbelieving people can have high moral standards—sometimes higher than those who profess to know God. Why? Because nobody can escape the goodness of the One whose image he or she bears. God created us for goodness.

Morality has to do with right and wrong, but not everything in life is black and white. Some things are a matter of good, better, and best. God has equipped us to navigate through these areas as well by endowing us with an appreciation for beauty. We will discuss this in greater depth in chapter 4, but at this point we want to say that this also is a reflection of God's image. Anthony Hoekema says it well: "Our sense of beauty is a feeble reflection of the God who scatters beauty profusely over snow-crowned peaks, lake-jeweled valleys, and awe-inspiring sunsets."[13]

Knowing what is good and how to appreciate beauty is a powerful combination integral to carrying out God's intentions here. Without it we

---

11. Augustine wrote extensively about evil and concluded that evil is the absence of good. Think of rust on a car; the rust begins as a perversion of the car's metal and leads to the absence of that metal altogether. Likewise, evil does not exist of its own accord—otherwise we would have a problem explaining how the Creator of all things created evil. Rather, evil began as a perversion of God's good creation and leads to an absence of goodness altogether. Without good, there could be no evil.

12. Our culture has tried to do away with "absolutes," blurring the lines between good and evil. However, we still find ourselves innately labeling things as "evil"—like the September 11 terrorist attacks—even though a world without absolutes has no grounds to do so. For an insightful perspective on this cultural (and human) phenomenon and how it relates to evangelism in today's anything-goes culture, note Harry Lee Poe's *See No Evil* in the additional resources at the end of chapter 5.

13. Hoekema, *Created in God's Image*, 71.

risk operating solely out of rational ability—making decisions based on whether or not something "solves a problem." Morality and an appreciation for beauty require that we also ask questions like, How will human life be affected by this decision? Will this be good for the ecosystem? Will this contribute to the beauty of the world God has made? Our sense of what is good and what is beautiful provide the counterbalance for our ability to reason. Developing and bettering God's world means we must always consider whether our actions benefit or harm people and the planet. It means we are concerned about making the world a more beautiful place. Anything less does not do justice to the reputation and character of the One we represent.

Accountability—Created for Dependence

We are rational, moral, aesthetic beings, all reflections of God's image in us. But none of this was given to us for ourselves. Because we bear God's image, we are accountable to Him. In a well-known New Testament story, a group sent by the Pharisees asks Jesus about paying taxes (Matt 22:15–21). In response He asks them whose face is on the coins in question. "Caesar's" is the answer. Jesus' famous response, "Render therefore unto Caesar the things which are Caesar's; and unto God the things that are Gods" (22:21 KJV) is often used as grudging proof that we should indeed pay Uncle Sam what he asks (demands) of us every year. This is true enough, but it misses the larger point Jesus was making. Coins bear the image of political rulers, and thus, belong to them. People, however, bear another image—God's—and thus, belong to Him.

Belonging to God means that we will ultimately answer to Him for our lives—how we used the abilities He gave us: abilities to think rationally, recognize good, and appreciate beauty. We will also answer for how we use the individual gifts He has given us: gifts of words, mathematical ability, musical talent, and countless other abilities.

Accountability is based on the fact that God created us with wills to choose. He created us for the purpose of using our wills to do His—and thus glorify Him—but He does not force us. From the very beginning, He has given humanity the freedom to choose obedience or disobedience. Even this ability to choose is part of imaging God because it reflects "the supreme directing power of him 'who works out everything in conformity with the purpose of his will' (Eph 1:11)."[14]

---

14. Ibid.

In God's original design, image-bearers used their gifts in harmony with God's will for them, but Adam and Eve's choice to disobey upset this harmony. Now humans, still image-bearers with God-given abilities and gifts, use these gifts against Him and against His desires for His creation. Herein lies one of sin's greatest tragedies: "Man is now using God-given and God-imaging powers to do things that are an affront to his maker."[15] The created chooses to work against the Creator.

In summary being an image-bearer means we are made for community, we are given responsibilities by God, and we will answer to God for our lives. Our abilities and the way we use them to relate to God and other people are among the most important things we do as humans. Do we use every aspect of our lives in the service of God and fellow human beings or do we use our lives against God and fellow human beings?

Jesus, the Fullness of God's Image

Because God's image in humankind has been so severely marred by sin, we sometimes have a hard time knowing what it looks like to live as God intended. Adam and Eve aren't much help in this quest since we barely get a glimpse of their perfection before it disappears. What does humanity in all its fullness look like?

The first Adam may not be much help, but the second Adam (or the last Adam; see Rom 5 and 1 Cor 15) succeeds where His predecessor fails. Jesus, the second Adam, shows us exactly what it means to live human life as God intended.

Jesus was fully divine, but He wasn't some kind of superhero who pulled out magic powers when He got in a bind. He was completely human, and when He took on human form, He left the glories of heaven behind. He sunk His feet into our mud, blistered His hands doing our tasks, and probably endured a headache or two from the press of people in His life.

He was human, but His was a humanity without sin. He was the perfect and full image of the invisible God (Col 1:15). By looking at Him, we can begin to understand the fullness of what it means for us to be created in the image of God. "In Christ . . . we see clearly what is hidden in Genesis 1: namely, what man as the perfect image of God should be like."[16]

And what do we see when we look at Jesus? Most simply, we see a man in right relationship with God, others, and creation. He obeyed

---

15. Ibid., 72.
16. Ibid., 73.

God, loved people, and ruled over nature. Jesus never wavered from His commitment to do the will of the Father, even though it led to the cross. He cared for people by teaching the multitudes, healing the sick, feeding the hungry, raising the dead, eating with sinners, and casting out demons. He ruled over nature by calming the sea, multiplying bread and fishes, and turning water into wine for the benefit of His followers.

What does it mean to bear God's image? Look at Jesus. We reflect God within the same three relationships. As totally dependent creatures, we should respond to God with joyful obedience, finding our satisfaction in Him. As social beings, we need each other as much as we need food and water, and God made us to serve and care for each other. Finally, we have the responsibility to tend and guard the natural world, finding its resources, cultivating its soil, and using its food for our well-being while carefully preserving it for generations yet to come.

Left to ourselves we cannot do this because we are fallen people. Because of sin's pervasiveness, we choose our own way instead of reflecting God in these three relationships. We ignore God (which is the same as disobedience), use others for our own benefit, and exploit the earth's resources.

Again, Jesus provides the remedy. Not only does He show us the perfect image of God, He redeems us so we can ultimately become the perfect image of God, too. Through Jesus and the miracle of the new birth, our hearts are renewed through faith in the atoning sacrifice of Jesus on the cross. The Holy Spirit becomes the agent of change in the believer's heart desires, goals, and actions—and He prompts Christians to use their abilities in the service of God and others.

Perfect restoration of God's image in us will not be realized until God makes a new heaven and a new earth, where the redeemed will live permanently (Rev 21:1–4; 22:14–15). We will finally relate to God and to each other in perfect ways. "The threefold relationship for which man was created will be maintained, deepened and infinitely enriched. We shall then love God above all, love our neighbors as ourselves, and rule over creation in a totally God-glorifying way. The image of God in man will then have been perfected."[17]

Maranatha! Even so come, Lord Jesus!

Basic Human Relationships and Responsibilities

Each of us is involved in an endless array of human relationships—we are spouses, parents, friends, neighbors, employees, church members, citizens,

---

17. Ibid., 95.

customers, and the list goes on. We are limiting our discussion to the three relationships upon which every society is built: husband-wife, parent-child, and "slave-master" (or the more politically correct "employer-employee"). Each of these relationships comes with its unique responsibilities, but the biblical principles for them can be applied to many other human relationships.[18]

Husband-Wife Relationship

> The man said,
> "This is now bone of my bones
>   and flesh of my flesh;
> she shall be called 'woman,'
>   for she was taken out of man."
> For this reason a man will leave his father and mother and be united to his wife, and they will become one flesh. (Gen 2:23–24)

Adam and Eve formed the first and most basic human relationship: husband and wife. Their relationship blossomed into a parent-to-child relationship that in turn created a brother-to-brother relationship. From this simple beginning, the population increased and the possibilities for human relationships multiplied (Gen 4:3–5:32).

As already suggested, the oneness and fellowship of husband and wife mirrors the oneness and fellowship of God the Father, God the Son, and God the Holy Spirit. In our sinful condition, this imaging of God is faulty at best. Those who attempt to fulfill the goal struggle between the ideal and the real but may, in some small measure, truly reflect the image of God in their marriage relationship.

Marriage also reflects God's creative capacity. Just as God created man in His image, now man and woman create little men and women in *their* image. God made man and woman to join together so they could fulfill the command to be fruitful and multiply and fill the earth. God intended that husbands and wives reproduce their own kind so they could populate and subdue the wonderful earth that He created.

Marriage and its role in imaging God received a boost after the redeeming work of Jesus Christ. Those who have been redeemed have the

---

18. Each relationship is, most importantly, contingent on our relationship with God. When asked to identify the greatest commandment, Jesus responded, "Love the Lord your God with all your heart and with all your soul and with all your mind" (Matt 22:37–38). All human relationships begin here—and the measure of our love for and commitment to God determines the quality of all our relationships.

ability to more fully image God. Paul gives instructions to that end in Ephesians 5:21–33:

> Submit to one another out of reverence for Christ. Wives, submit to your husbands as to the Lord. For the husband is the head of the wife as Christ is the head of the church, his body, of which he is the Savior. Now as the church submits to Christ, so also wives should submit to their husbands in everything.
>
> Husbands, love your wives, just as Christ loved the church and gave himself up for her to make her holy, cleansing her by the washing with water through the word, and to present her to himself as a radiant church, without stain or wrinkle or any other blemish, but holy and blameless. In this same way, husbands ought to love their wives as their own bodies. . . . Each one of you also must love his wife as he loves himself, and the wife must respect her husband.

Three key words characterize this passage: submit, respect, and love. The wife submits to and respects her husband, and the husband loves his wife. The husband is the head of the relationship, a position and responsibility given him at the beginning by God. The wife is to yield to his loving leadership and consider her submission to him the same as being submissive to Christ. The husband has an equal—and perhaps even greater—responsibility in loving his wife in the same way that Christ loved the church.

The ideal is easy to explain, but the real is difficult to attain. We are sinners and we each desire to be in charge. How well the ideal biblical relationship works out in any marriage depends on each partner, what they bring to the relationship from their backgrounds, their submission to Christ's headship over them, and their willingness to continually work toward the ideal. Marriage is a two-partner effort. Both must assume their roles and responsibilities, otherwise the relationship will stumble.

Another key ingredient in a successful marriage is that of faithfulness. God sets the example in His continual sustaining of the seasons, days and nights, adequate food, beautiful sunsets and sunrises. And although He also allows storms, disasters, sicknesses, and death, we can nonetheless count on God to help when we cry out to Him. In a similar way, husbands and wives are to be "glued" to each other, no matter what circumstances arise. Faithfulness means sticking with each other through the stormy times as well as through the sunny times, and it provides confidence in each other's behavior whether together or apart.

Parent-Child Relationship

> Children, obey your parents in the Lord, for this is right. "Honor your father and mother"—which is the first commandment with a promise—"that it may go well with you and that you may enjoy long life on the earth." Fathers, do not exasperate your children; instead bring them up in the training and instruction of the Lord. (Eph 6:1–4, citing Exod 20:12)

Conceiving children is easy and often accidental or incidental, but rearing children is one of the most difficult—and important—tasks parents undertake. The challenge is to love and nurture them to adulthood, and there are no easy ways.

Like the husband-wife relationship, parent-child relationships are also a two-way street where each has certain responsibilities. Scripture has many admonitions and instructions for parents and children, but the passage cited above provides a critical framework.

Children are commanded to obey, submitting to their parents' instructions, commands, and counsel. The degree to which they put themselves under their parents' authority indicates the degree to which they also submit to God.

Parents are instructed to teach and model behaviors and attitudes that children need for life. Without even trying, parents model life behaviors—good and bad. The Bible admonishes them to teach and instruct their children in the Lord (Deut 6:4–9; Eph 6:4). Teaching children during their first years of life is done daily as parents love them, speak to them, and care for them. As children grow, parents teach by talking about and encouraging right behaviors. They read to their children and talk about the world around them to develop their language. They talk about God and His love for children, and they model His love in their care and treatment of their children.

The Bible also instructs parents, especially fathers, not to exasperate their children (Eph 6:4), and Colossians 3:21 explains why: "Fathers, do not embitter your children, or they will become discouraged." Expectations must not be so difficult that children always fall short of success. As children succeed, the bar can be slowly raised commensurate with age and ability. Continual failure to meet expectations results in discouragement and anger toward the parents. Punishment for disobedience must be appropriate and not harsh and arbitrary, or the spirit of the child will be broken.

Although parenting carries no guarantees, the likely result of proper instruction and responsive obedience is that children will develop a lifelong respect for their parents. Anthony Tomasino says of parents: "We're to hold them in proper respect, recognizing the hierarchy of creation that made our parents our predecessors and acknowledging the debt we owe to them for rearing us."[19] He then talks about the need for children to become the love givers and nurturers of their parents when they age and become dependent: "We depended utterly on them for nurture, for warmth, and for love. And now, who do they have to depend on but us?"[20]

Parents will always view their children as their children, even when they mature, marry, rear families, support themselves, and interact as adults. Parents want to be proud of their children because they carry the family values into their own families and communities. Proverbs 17:6 captures the long view of parent-child relationships: "Children's children are a crown to the aged, and parents are the pride of their children." May that be the goal and prize of every family.

Employer-Employee Relationships

Families and individuals need to have resources to maintain their existence, and these resources are usually obtained through working for someone or running a personal business. The Bible has much to say about the relationships between employers and employees.

> Slaves, obey your earthly masters with respect and fear, and with sincerity of heart, just as you would obey Christ. Obey them not only to win their favor when their eye is on you, but like slaves of Christ, doing the will of God from your heart. Serve wholeheartedly, as if you were serving the Lord, not men, because you know that the Lord will reward everyone for whatever good he does, whether he is slave or free. And masters, treat your slaves in the same way. Do not threaten them, since you know that he who is both their master and yours is in heaven, and there is no favoritism with him. (Eph 6:5–9)

Adam was the first person to be assigned work, and contrary to popular belief, it was *not* part of the curse. He was assigned to work the garden (Gen 2:15) because even in a perfect world, plants had to be cultivated, pruned, and harvested. The entrance of sin into the world is what complicated things; Adam had to work the earth "by the sweat of his brow,"

---

19. Tomasino, *Written Upon the Heart*, 103.
20. Ibid., 107.

fighting weeds and other environmental enemies (Gen 3:17–19). While most of us do not do what Adam did for a living, we nonetheless fight sin's effects in every aspect of the environment.

What exactly is work? Most simply, it is physical or mental activity that results in something being accomplished. Work is part of our responsibility to fill, rule, and subdue the earth. While work is often difficult, tiresome, monotonous, and even dangerous, God intends it to be fulfilling, challenging, exhilarating, and rewarding. Work is our partnership with God in caring for this planet and uncovering the many wonders hidden in it that can improve and enhance our lives.

Work is also the way we provide for personal and family needs, a responsibility the Apostle Paul takes seriously in his letter to Timothy: "If anyone does not provide for his relatives, and especially for his immediate family, he has denied the faith and is worse than an unbeliever" (1 Tim 5:8). Unless we are unable to work, God intends that we provide for ourselves and demonstrate love for our families by working. Paul's sharp words to some lazy Thessalonians still ring true today: "If a man will not work, he shall not eat" (2 Thess 3:10).

Whether working for a Christian or non-Christian, employees who are followers of Jesus are to fulfill their responsibilities enthusiastically, demonstrating a genuine interest in the success of the business. Employees are to show respect and deference to their supervisors, following their instructions as if Christ Himself were giving them. Sincere, humble, enthusiastic service is a powerful testimony of the power of God to change lives. Paul declares that those who work in this way are really doing the will of God (Eph 6:6–7).

Employers are responsible to meet the needs of their workers and treat them with respect, also recognizing that they are serving Christ in the way they treat employees. While their responsibility to protect company assets means they must enforce company policies and administer discipline when policies are not followed, supervisors are to discipline in love and with respect—in just the way the supervisor would want to be disciplined by God.

Employers are also responsible to remunerate employees with a fair wage and benefits, allowing them to share in the prosperity of the business when it is feasible (Col 4:1). The employer needs to provide a safe and adequate work environment, all necessary equipment, and reasonable expectations.

Relationships, encountered in every facet of life, are foundational to what it means to bear the image of God. We honor God by respecting, loving, and serving others—first at home and then in every other relationship.

People and School Subjects

Cultures have been built on the relationships described above since the beginning of time. The role of social studies in the Christian school is to help students understand how these relationships and the ones that grow from them have shaped our world. Its role is also to prepare them to take their place responsibly in this world.

We each eventually leave the comforts of our homes to become part of the larger culture of communities, states, nations, and the world. Each of these has its own structure that children begin learning about when they enter the classroom and relate to other authority figures and classmates. As they move through the grades they learn to be a part of the small, temporary community of their class within the larger community of their school. Simultaneously, they are "officially" learning about community relationships through history, government, geography, and economics.

Unfortunately, too often these courses are seen as boring, and students are unaware (or unconcerned) that social studies are the outcome of the responsibilities God assigned to people at creation. Social studies comprise the story of sinful people managing the wonderful planet He created for us. Each person, family, people group, and nation has its own history and each is part of the larger history of its culture and of all of mankind.

History—Remembering, and Not Repeating

History tells us how well people have fulfilled the creation commands to fill the earth and subdue it (Gen 1:28). The record of this is admittedly not very pretty—and should be a continual reminder to us of our need for God's redemption, a plan that occurs within the context of history. Empires and leaders rise and fall in an endless progression of historical events precipitated by human lust for power. Masses of humanity are often abused, killed, displaced, or enslaved as power seekers compete for control. History should make indisputably clear to our students that what God saw in the days of Noah is still true today: every inclination of the thoughts of people's hearts is evil all the time (Gen 6:5). These patterns of behavior will continue to be evident in history until the final judgments described in Revelation 20–22.

God has given us a history lesson par excellence in the development of His chosen people, Israel. They serve as a perfect example of the importance of history—remembering the past.

God made a covenant with Israel, promising to be their ruler, protector, and God as long as they lived up to the terms of the covenant established in the Ten Commandments and a host of other laws governing interpersonal relationships. In the book of Deuteronomy, forty years after Israel's deliverance from Egypt, Moses rehearses the history of the people before they enter the Promised Land. A key word in Moses' Deuteronomy speeches is *remember*: remember significant events God did on the journey from Mount Sinai to Moab; remember the commandments and impress them upon your children; remember, remember, remember.

The remainder of the Old Testament is the record of the people's forgetting and the prophets' call to remember. As the people take possession of the land and live in it for hundreds of years, they cycle through periods of obedience, disobedience, repression, repentance, and deliverance. They forget what God did for them and instead want to be like the nations around them. Their failure to remember costs them their nation, their land, and their identity for many years.

God wanted Israel to remember the past, including its mistakes, so they would hopefully not repeat them. They needed to remember who they were as a people and whose they were. They needed continual reminding of who God was and why they were to worship only Him at a prescribed place in a prescribed manner with a proper attitude. The religions of their neighbors were very inviting, and their women were so beautiful and their men so handsome that it was difficult to be content with a Jewish spouse and worship the Holy God in the assigned location offering the best of their flocks and crops. They failed to remember, and they paid the price.

How does this apply to us today? We live in a country where we enjoy many freedoms. We have a government that has checks and balances, a feature that is not true among most nations and which is the envy of much of the world. We must remember how we got to this point and how we have had to fight to preserve our heritage. History is an important subject to study so that our past is not forgotten in challenges to its efficacy. Remember Moses and his review of Israel's brief but significant history and read Deuteronomy often.

Government—Keeping Control and Working for the Greatest Good

God's commands to rule, fill, and subdue the earth necessitated the development of structures—beginning with the family and extending to world governments—so the tasks could be fulfilled in an orderly manner, ensuring that the earth's resources would be made available to all and that law and order would be upheld to protect people.

Government is ordained by God, and we are obligated to obey its laws and regulations (Rom 13:1–7). Jesus was in submission to the Roman government of His day (Matt 22:21), and Paul echoed Jesus' teaching when he said, "This is also why you pay taxes, for the authorities are God's servants, who give their full time to governing. Give everyone what you owe him: If you owe taxes, pay taxes; if revenue, pay revenue; if respect, then respect; if honor, then honor" (Rom 13:6–7).

There are many different forms of government in the world, but God has not established nor put His stamp of approval on any one form of government. Nations have the freedom to create their governmental structure so that all people can feel safe and can have a share in the country's goods and services. Sin rears its ugly head here, and tyrannical governments oppress people and often keep them in poverty while the leaders enrich themselves. Just as between individuals, relationships between nations can be friendly and cooperative, but they can also become strained and broken. Diplomacy might solve the differences, but often governments resort to fighting and killing.

In addition to obedience, those of us who are followers of Jesus Christ and who have a strong faith in God need to pray for governmental leadership: "I urge, then, first of all, that requests, prayers, intercession and thanksgiving be made for everyone—for kings and all those in authority, that we may live peaceful and quiet lives in all godliness and holiness" (1 Tim 2:1–2). When granted, this request allows us the freedom to image God in all of our relationships without being subject to arrest and punishment.

Respecting and obeying government is part of a larger issue, that of being good citizens wherever we live. Involvement in the community is an important part of living out God's values as we demonstrate compassion for our neighbors and interest in the issues that affect us and those around us.

Geography—Knowing and Appreciating Our Neighbors

Everybody lives somewhere, either on land or in a boat on the water or maybe even under a rock, and a person's physical surroundings shape her view of the world and the development of her culture. Someone living along a major river, a waterway of commerce, will have different experiences than someone growing up in an isolated rural area. The resulting diversity of peoples and cultures has made the population of this world a beautiful potpourri of customs, languages, and contributions to the monumental responsibility of subduing this planet.

Continents, oceans, large countries and cities, rivers and mountain ranges, plains and river valleys are all part of the larger picture, so often difficult to see because we are consumed by our immediate surroundings. As people spread around the planet after the tower of Babel, they had to become creative and adaptable to eke out a living in the hard places: sandy, snowy, rocky, and marshy. To fully understand a people, we have to understand their immediate physical environment. Learning about the physical features of the planet and the ways they have affected people groups is an important part of being a good global citizen.

Economics—Stewarding Our Resources

Adam's initial assignment from God was to work the garden and take care of it (Gen 2:15). After the fall, God told Adam that he, through lifelong painful and sweaty toil, would work the sin-cursed soil to get food. His son Cain was a farmer and Abel was a shepherd. Later Cain was an architect, constructing a city. His descendents were farmers, metal smiths, and instrumentalists (Gen 4:19–22). Those who produced food exchanged with those who made tools, and both shared with the one who made musical instruments so all could play lilting melodies for listening pleasure and to sooth weary minds and bodies at the end of a day of sweaty toil. Economics was born.

Sharing products and skills involves trading, bartering, and selling. As co-regents of the earth, people have the responsibility to care for the earth's resources, intended for the benefit of all earth's inhabitants. Men and women are stewards of God's creation, commanded to make sure that everyone receives his portion, that the resources are not wasted, and that the landscape is not ruined. Stewardship ought to be the biblical principle that drives economics—not personal gain, power, and prestige.

Like nearly everything else, stewardship and economics begin at home as each person and family use their resources to provide for their needs as well as return God's portion to Him. But stewardship and economics also are taught in school, beginning in the earliest grades as students use school property with care, earn and save money for classroom projects, and develop projects to help those in need.

Conclusion

Relating to people can be one of the most difficult things we do since each person is unique in personality, ability, and interests—all significant aspects of image bearing. But relating to people is also one of the most fundamental things we do—fundamental to our nature as image-bearers and fundamental to existence in a world populated by people! Helping our students understand people from the context of social studies is vital for their development into responsible members of families, churches, communities, and the world.

Summary of Truths

In this chapter we have discussed the significance of being created in God's image and how this truth affects the way we view the world and its population.

Bearing His Image

1. Human beings, created with similarities to many creatures, stand apart from them through being made like God Himself.
2. Humans, created in the image of God, are like God in some of His attributes: rationality, morality, fellowship, will, and appreciation of beauty.
3. Sin perverted the image of God in man so people now use their God-endowed gifts and abilities against God and fellow human beings.
4. Jesus demonstrated, in His incarnation as the God-man, how the image of God in us should be manifested.
5. The perverted image can be partially restored through the new birth, thereby allowing gifts and abilities to be used for God and fellow human beings.
6. The image will be fully restored in the new heaven and the new earth where the redeemed will be able to relate to God, to each other, and to nature in perfect ways.
7. God created people as relational creatures to relate to Him and to each other.

Relating to Others

1. Relationships begin with the recognition that we are dependent upon God for life and for the sustaining of it.
2. The fundamental human relationship is that of the marriage of a man and a woman, and it images the fellowship within the Godhead.

3. Parent-child relationships, the fruit of marriage, image the love relationship of God with His children. The bearing of children fulfills the creation command to multiply and fill the earth.

4. Work was assigned to Adam before sin entered the world; it images God and is incumbent upon all of us.

Understanding the Subject Matter

1. History is the study of sinful people fulfilling God's creation commands to fill, rule, and subdue.

2. History is studied so we remember who we are, what it took to bring us to this point, and how we should move forward.

3. Governmental structures have been ordained by God and are necessary to insure fair treatment of all citizens, to uphold law and order, and to insure fair and equitable distribution of the earth's resources.

4. The study of geography will help us appreciate God's sovereign placement of land and water and how location has given uniqueness to each people group and culture.

5. As God's co-regents in subduing the earth, humankind has a solemn responsibility to make wise and conservative use of earth's resources, natural and manufactured, for the benefit of all mankind. This is called economics and stewardship.

Teaching Tips

1. All for One and One for All. Take your class on a silent tour of your school building (or brainstorm in the classroom); have them observe, without speaking, all the different people and what they are doing. When you return to the classroom, have them write (still silently) as many people as they remember and what they were doing. (If you want to speed things up, make this a class activity together.) Ask your students what they learned from observing all the different people/tasks. You are guiding them to say that it takes many different people doing many different jobs to make the school run. You can expand on this and talk about other places. Also guide them to talk about people doing things they are good at, and what might happen if people's jobs were all mixed up. Use portions of 2 Corinthians 12:12–27 to help your students understand that "many people, many gifts" is God's

idea. Wendy has a friend who used the catchy phrase "If I were a sixth-grade eyeball . . . " (with a very fun visual) to help her older students work with this idea. (Lower elementary grades; with variation, upper elementary)

2. Inheriting Life. Have your students interview their grandparents (if some students do not have accessible grandparents or "stand-ins," pair or group students so they each have a connection to someone who is not a total stranger), asking a list of questions about their lives growing up: construct a list for them to use that will especially highlight the changes from then to now. Make sure your list also highlights things that do not change (how grandparents felt about certain things, etc.). Then have your students interview their parents, asking the same questions. In class, talk about the similarities and differences, and guide the discussion to help your students see how much the world changes but how much people still have in common. (Lower elementary; with variation, upper elementary)

3. It's *Not* All About Me. The importance of understanding different people groups, cultures, and history is directly applicable to understanding the Bible. It was written in a vastly different terrain, radically different culture, and far-removed time. Yet, we often read it like a "straight shot" from the authors' hands to our eyes. This leads to incredibly inconsistent reading of the Bible. For example, how do you decide which commands are for you and which are not? (Just try reading Lev 19:18–19 and explaining to your class why it *is* important to love our neighbors as ourselves [v 18], but *not* important to worry about clothing made of mixed materials [v 19].) Sometimes with the Bible this can be dangerous and sometimes it is just nonsensical. With the use of commentaries and other biblical study materials, engage your class in the study of the parables with an eye to understanding what they meant in that culture and time. Have your students read parables without the use of any study helps and venture interpretations of them. Then have them work through the cultural issues and revise their interpretation.

After this exercise (perhaps an assignment over several days' time), move into contemporary life and focus on how properly understanding people today depends on understanding their location and culture. The reality of "ugly Americans," in part, grows out of our failure to understand people groups. There is ample opportunity in current events to raise this issue. (High school)

4. **Living in the Real World.** This simulation will help your students understand some basic economic ideas, as well as some factors that led to the Great Depression. It will also reveal to them their own greed, a very important concept in the Bible. Set up a system of "cash earnings" in your classroom, and make some fake cash to carry out the simulation. Inform your students that they are all employees in your company (name it something fun), and you will "pay" them for their work (homework, participation, classroom tasks, offering extra help, etc.). Likewise, they will have to "pay" for things like desk rental, late homework, extra long (or loud) restroom breaks, etc. (You are the designated collector of the money, but it is all money "for the company"; i.e., you are not "getting rich" off their rent!) Compile a list of ways they can "spend" their money: free assignment, extra recess, and other privileges.

   After doing this for a few days, introduce the idea of buying shares in your company. Explain how the concept of purchasing shares works: when the company makes money, they make money; when the company loses, they lose. Each day announce how the company did overnight and pay dividends as appropriate. Then have a time when they can buy/sell shares. It works best if you let the students make a decent amount of money and only lose a little. They will get overconfident and lead beautifully into the day you announce that your company has gone bankrupt. Their shares are worthless, and as their employer, you are bankrupt, too. They will receive no more money, but they still have to pay for everything as before. Some students will be instantly broke, and the next few days of the simulation will prove interesting and educational as the students learn how to survive. (In Wendy's class, this activity coincided with a unit on the Depression, so the bankrupt students lost their desks and had to move into a "Hooverville"; actually, she let them still sit in the desks, but they had to store all their belongings in a box and carry it everywhere they went.) Use the simulation to reinforce basic concepts about the economy, as well as about greed. Be sure to use the ninth commandment (Exod 20:17), the "love of money" (1 Tim 6:10), Jesus' parable about storing up treasures (Matt 6:19–21), and the story of the rich fool (Luke 12:16–21). You can also use the opportunity to talk about poverty (and the Christian's response to it; a project of raising money for a local mission or the like would fit well at the end of this simulation), trusting God to care for our needs, and stewardship. The simulation creates a wonderful atmosphere for a host of biblical concepts. The instructions here are a basic sketch to get you started; you will have to develop many of the details for your own class. (Upper elementary grades, junior high)

5. Standing on Their Shoulders. Each generation adds to the learning of previous generations (we "stand on their shoulders"), and it is important for our students to appreciate the history that leads to present-day disciplines. Compile a list of Christians who have worked in your subject area, and as part of your semester's assigned workload, have students read a biography of a Christian in your field and report in writing or to the class what the person accomplished, how faith influenced his or her studies, and what legacy he or she has left. (Junior high and high school)

Additional Resources[21]

1. Black, Amy E. *Beyond Left and Right: Helping Christians Make Sense of American Politics.* Grand Rapids: Baker Books, 2008. The target audience for this book is an educated lay reader who may not remember the details of high school or college civics but wants to know more about participating in American government.

2. Daniell, David. *The Bible in English: Its History and Influence.* New Haven, CT: Yale University Press, 2003. Daniell is an engaging writer who minces no words when telling his readers how important the English Bible has been since Wycliff and Tyndale translated the Scriptures into English.

3. DiIulio, John J. *Godly Republic: A Centrist Blueprint for America's Faith-Based Future.* Berkeley: University of California Press, 2007. A one-time member of the Bush administration, DiIulio enters the debate over whether America is a Christian or secular nation, and to what degree the separation of church and state is compelled by the Constitution.

4. Gaustad, Edwin S. *Proclaim Liberty Throughout All the Land: A History of Church and State in America.* New York: Oxford, 2003. In this book about religion and American history, Gaustad traces the complicated relationship of church and state from the colonial period to the modern day.

5. Jenkins, Philip. *The Next Christendom: The Coming of Global Christianity.* Oxford: Oxford University Press, 2002. This book will challenge readers to

---

21. Thanks to Keith Widder, Kelly Fath, and Amy Black for their help compiling this diverse list.

see the contemporary church in broader global view than most evangelical Christians living in the U. S. normally do.

6. Kemeny, P. C., ed. *Church, State, and Public Justice: Five Views.* Downers Grove, IL: InterVarsity Academic, 2007. This book presents five views (Catholic, classical Baptist, evangelical Anabaptist, Reformed principled pluralism, mainline Protestant) on the relationship between the church and government and is instructive for sorting out an appropriate corporate and personal response to social issues.

7. Land, Richard. *The Divided States of America? What Liberals AND Conservatives Are Missing in the God-and-Country Shouting Match!* Nashville: Thomas Nelson, 2007. Land writes this popular book from the ideological right, looking at the separation of church and state: what it is, what it isn't, and why it matters for the future of religion in America.

8. Noll, Mark A. *Turning Points: Decisive Moments in the History of Christianity.* Grand Rapids: Baker Books, 1997. Noll wrote this book as an aid to teach a class in church history in his church. It can inform a teacher as to the importance of the history of the church and its significance in the history of the world since the resurrection.

9. Sider, Ronald J., and Dianne Knippers, eds. *Toward an Evangelical Public Policy: Political Strategies for the Health of the Nation.* Grand Rapids: Baker Books, 2005. While evangelicals are flooding into politics, they often do so without a carefully developed biblical framework for involvement. This book is designed to deepen their understanding of political involvement, as well as unify and strengthen the presence of evangelicals in politics.

10. Wallis, Jim. *God's Politics: Why the Right Gets It Wrong and the Left Doesn't Get It.* San Francisco: Harper, 2005. Writing from the ideological left, Wallis proposes a new sort of politics in which the distance between right and left can be bridged for the betterment of society.

3

──────── Communication ────────

Did you ever wonder who invented Show and Tell? What elementary school teacher decided the Friday afternoon ritual of introducing pet rocks, displaying lost teeth, and admiring foreign currency was important? And how did he or she convince the rest of the world that revolves around such important matters as readin', writin', and 'rithmatic that sharing artifacts from home is time well spent?

We don't have the foggiest idea who invented it, but we suspect they intuitively understood one of the most fundamental aspects of human personality—the need to connect with other people. We need to share what's important to us, to be appreciated and enjoyed for who we are, and to be part of other people's lives in the same way.

This "connecting" is present all day long in school. Hastily scrawled notes slip across aisles; secret playground languages transmit critical third-grade news; raspy whispers break the silence of study hall. We are bursting to express ourselves—even the quietest among us; we journal, doodle, text-message, show photographs, tell jokes, write stories, play games. Communication is as much a part of our nature as breathing; we can't not do it.

At its most basic level, communication is the exchange of information, the sending and receiving of data. When as teachers we ignore a roomful of yawns and press on in our explanations of the differences between *affect* and *effect*, *it's* and *its*, and satire and journalism, we do it so our students will be the best senders and receivers they can be. We labor over appositives, diagramming, vocabulary words, poetry, persuasive speeches, business letters, and oral book reports because we want our students to have something to say and to say it well.

But communication is much more than merely sending and receiving information; communication is the expression of ourselves. Because we are living, breathing image-bearers with opinions, interests, and personalities, we cannot send and receive information without including ourselves in it. That's why newscasts are biased, stories have an angle, and eyewitnesses see different events; it's why Johnny misses his mother's instructions about taking out the trash but clearly hears her say Chuck E. Cheese's is for dinner.

Communication

In biblical terms, communication is the overflow of our hearts; who we are inside shows in our verbal and non-verbal expressions. In everything we say or write, we show who we are, and in everything we hear or read, we receive who others are. Thus, while one of the tasks of educators is to produce good senders and receivers—that is, students who are able to discern what is worthwhile in what they read and hear, and to speak and write in ways that are clear and appropriate—the underlying task of Christian educators is to help our students be the most godly people they can be so the "overflow" of their hearts clearly expresses love for God, love for people, and care of His creation. Language arts are the way we help students package and deliver the "overflow" of the heart.

Introduction

WHEN HELEN Keller was nineteen months old, a mysterious fever "closed [her] eyes and ears and plunged [her] into the unconsciousness of a newborn baby."[1] The silence and darkness trapped her in a world of crude and inadequate communication—touching others' lips to know what they were saying and using pantomime to signal what she needed or wanted. It's no wonder Helen was frustrated: "The desire to express myself grew. . . . I felt as if invisible hands were holding me and I made frantic efforts to free myself."[2] In these "frantic efforts" to escape her imprisonment, an out-of-control Helen held her family captive as well.

And then came the now famous Anne Sullivan, Helen's long-suffering teacher who opened the world to her difficult student by teaching her to communicate effectively. She taught her to see through her blindness, hear through her deafness, and speak through her muteness. She opened the channels of sending and receiving that the fever had closed.

Helen's "eureka" moment and foray into the world of clear, worthwhile, and appropriate communication came one morning at the water pump:

> As the cool stream gushed over one hand [Anne] spelled into the other the word *water*, first slowly, then rapidly. I stood still, my whole attention fixed on the motions of her fingers. Suddenly I felt a misty consciousness as of something forgotten—a thrill of returning thought; and somehow the mystery of language was revealed to me. I knew then that "w-a-t-e-r" meant the wonderful cool something that was flowing over my hand. That living word

---

1. Keller, *Helen Keller: The Story of My Life*, 13.
2. Ibid., 18

awakened my soul, gave it light, hope, joy, set it free! . . . Everything had a name, and each name gave birth to a new thought.[3]

Until she was nearly seven years old, Helen Keller exemplified the intellectual anemia and emotional frustration that result when verbal reception and expression are impaired. She was living but not really *alive* because, on a most fundamental level, we were created to communicate. We were made in the likeness of God who *spoke* the world into existence, *expressed* Himself to humanity in a variety of ways including *writing* a Book, and ultimately sent the Living *Word* to this planet to make Himself fully known. God is a communicating God; we, in His image, are communicators, too.

Communication—What It Is

Communication, specifically language ability, comprises one of the most vital and unique aspects of humanity. While creatures like dolphins, birds, and chimpanzees communicate, only humans have language ability. In complex ways that linguists cannot explain, we are born with the ability to arrange an infinite number of words in the right order to produce an infinite number of sentences. We are able to process words and sentences, even jumbled ones. Take this example from an around-the-world Internet message:

> I cdnuolt blveiee taht I cluod aulaclty uesdnatnrd waht I was rdanieg. The phaonmneal pweor of the hmuan mnid. Aoccdrnig to rscheearch at Cmabrigde Uinervtisy, it deosn't mttaer in waht oredr the ltteers in a wrod are, the olny iprmoatnt tihng is taht the frist and lsat ltteer be in the rghit pclae. The rset can be a taotl mses and you can still raed it wouthit a porbelm. Tihs is bcuseae the huamn mnid deos not raed ervey lteter by istlef, but the wrod as a wlohe. Amzanig huh? yaeh and I awlyas thought slpeling was ipmorantt.

It's probably not a good idea to share this information with your elementary students who are laboring over this week's spelling list, but the implications of this example are mind-boggling, or in the words of the message, "phaonmneal." While we think spelling *is* important and don't suggest that you stop teaching it, we marvel at the capacity of the human mind to process words and meanings.

Our language ability is certainly one of our greatest assets and blessings from God, and its basic features are acquired with relative ease as parents talk to their children, name objects, read and listen to them.

---

3. Ibid., 21.

In all these things, parents are teaching, but anybody who has heard a child repeat an inappropriate word he overheard knows that language is more "caught" than taught. The ease with which children in particular "catch" language is evident by how rapidly they pick up a second language. Missionary children who grow up in a foreign culture learn the language faster in their interaction and play with other children than their parents acquire it after attending language school for months.

Communication begins with ideas in our minds and is expressed through language, written and spoken. I'm sitting at my desk as I compose these thoughts on my computer. I formulate a logical arrangement of paragraphs, each with a theme. In each paragraph, I formulate sentences to explain in the clearest way possible the theme that I want to communicate. At the end of a sentence, I read what I wrote and modify it as necessary to be sure the ideas in my head have found the right expression on paper (or computer screen).

For most of us, speech is the easier method of communicating ideas; we can spew out sentences faster than we can write them, and usually with much less effort. But the physiological processes of speaking and hearing are as complicated and miraculous as the ability to create ideas or write sentences. Ideas take shape vocally when air is forced out of the lungs, passes over the vocal cords, and produces a vibration. This vibrating air moves through the pharynx, oral cavity, and nasal cavity. The "simple" process of speaking requires the cooperation of the lungs, larynx, vocal cords, nasal passages, palate, tongue, teeth, and lips. If any of these is not functioning up to par, speech is impaired. You know this if you have tried to talk after dental work, when your nose is stuffed, or with a sore throat.

While your vocal cords process these vibrations, sound waves travel through the air to listening ears where another remarkable series of events is underway. The outer ear channels the sound waves into the auditory canal to the eardrum; the eardrum vibrates against three tiny bones, amplifying the vibrations into the inner ear where the cochlea picks them up; its fluid-filled canals are lined with hair-like nerve cells whose waving produces electrical impulses that feed into the auditory nerve which leads to the brain where they are unscrambled into sounds that we understand as words or speech. Whew! All that just to hear! And the miracle of it is that when these vibrating waves of air reach our brains, we understand them as words, sentences, and ideas. All of this happens with little or no effort.

As we have already suggested, communication is more than sending and receiving speech. The dictionary calls it the exchange of thoughts, opinions, or information through the use of speech, writing, or signs.

While this definition is helpful, it is lifeless. Communication is the stuff of life. We communicate because we want to share something—an event, an idea, a feeling, a story, a joke, or a warning. Communication is two junior high girls debating with each other whether the cutest guy in their class knows they're alive; it's young mothers sharing their experiences from labor and delivery; it's Tiger Woods tipping his cap to an applauding gallery after a birdie on the eighteenth hole; it's the third base coach waving the runner home; it's the want-to-be businessman working to persuade an investor that his plan is a good bet.

The need to communicate is so strong that we find ways to do it when the primary mode is blocked: students surreptitiously pass notes when the teacher forbids talking in class; young children pout and stick out their lower lips when told to not talk back; prisoners tap out messages on metal pipes; lighted lanterns hang in the steeple of Boston's Old North Church; and Helen Keller touches the faces of those around her. Just as we must inhale and exhale air, so we must receive and send expressions of *life*.

Modeled After the Master Communicator

Like everything else good about us, this ability and need to communicate—to know and to be known—comes from God. We are modeled after the Master Communicator, and although He does not need to share Himself with us, He has chosen to so we can enjoy Him too. God has delighted in Himself from eternity past. Medieval theologian Anselm of Canterbury called Him "that than which no greater can be thought." He is the greatest possible good, the very essence of delight. He didn't need us or anything in all creation to complete His delight, but because pure delight bubbles over, we should not be surprised that God created beings who could also enjoy Him.[4] In the same way but on a human level, He designed us to "bubble over," sharing ourselves with others and delighting in them. We reflect a God who has made Himself known to us in many different ways: He spoke, He wrote, and He came in the flesh.

God Spoke—Let There Be Light!

Through the natural world, God has communicated much about Himself. When you gaze into a night sky thick with stars, you can understand a little bit of God's vastness. Standing in the spray of thundering Niagara

---

4. This paragraph and the next are adapted from *A Match Made in Heaven: How Singles and the Church Can Live Happily Ever After* by Wendy Widder (Grand Rapids: Kregel Publications, 2003), 115–16.

Falls, you feel mere droplets of God's power. As you caress the perfect tiny fingers of a newborn, you can marvel at the tenderness of God. Immersing your face in a bouquet of flowers, you breathe in a little of God's beauty. In thousands of ways, God has shared Himself in creation.

Since we dealt extensively with this idea in chapter one, we will let you reference that chapter with the awareness that creation is the most obvious way God has communicated with us about Himself. But the natural world cannot explain His love and mercy; knowledge of these things can only come through God's words—Scripture—accompanied by His deeds.

God Wrote—the Greatest Story Ever Told

Although we see the evidence of God's spoken word all around us, none of us were there to hear Him speak at creation. We do, however, have a massive written collection of God's words. The Bible's sixty-six books comprise a record of His revelation, or for our purposes, His communication with people and their responses to Him.

The Bible is unique among books. God used forty human authors, each writing within the context of his personality and culture over a period of fifteen hundred years. Each author's work meshes with every other author's work to give a comprehensive and cohesive narrative. The Holy Spirit superintended the writing so no one writer could claim sole credit for having been the recipient of special revelation from God:

> And we have the word of prophecy made more certain, and you will do well to pay attention to it, as to a light shining in a dark place, until the day dawns and the morning star rises in your hearts. Above all, you must understand that no prophecy of Scripture came about by the prophet's own interpretation. For prophecy never had its origin in the will of man, but men spoke from God as they were carried along by the Holy Spirit. (2 Pet 1:19–21)

The greatest wonder of the Bible is that the Sovereign God has provided us with a personal word. He has not left us in a lurch wondering about Him, imagining what He is like, what He expects of us, and how can we relate to Him. Instead He has graciously and lovingly given us the truth about Himself along with clear instructions for living.

A secondary wonder of the Bible is its superb literary construction. The Bible really is the greatest Story ever told, but it is not a fictional story in any sense of the word. It is a factual account that God wove with strands of literary forms already in use in ancient times. It includes narrative, poetry, letters, prophecy, history, wisdom, and more. Those who consider the Bible a literary work—even if that's all they think it is—honor God because they admire *His* work, much like the naturalist scientist who marvels at the complexities of the natural world unknowingly honors the God who created it. Opponents of God and His Word may attack the divine nature or the theological concepts of the Bible, but they cannot fault its literary qualities. And because they read the very words of God, the Spirit who inspired these words can also lead them into truth and spiritual rebirth.

The Bible as Narrative

The largest percentage of the Bible is narrative, and while the combined narratives of the Bible make one grand and true Story, each operates on three levels. The lowest level consists of the hundreds of individual narratives, like the many events that make up the life of Abraham. The second level centers on the formation of Israel from its beginning to its ultimate restoration at the end of time. The third and highest level is the cosmic plan of God, or redemptive history—creation, the fall into sin, the working of God's redemptive plan through Jesus, and finally the new creation. The central person of every narrative, regardless of its level, is God.

Why did God choose narrative? Because stories draw us in; we cannot stop reading, listening, or watching because we want to know the outcome for the main character and vicariously for ourselves. We put ourselves in stories; with the Bible, this is exactly the point: we *are* part of the story of Scripture.

The Bible as Poetry

Much of the Bible—mostly in the Old Testament—is poetry. Poets create verbal images, like the shepherd in Psalm 23. When we think about a shepherd tending his flock on a hillside in Palestine, we understand in a richer way how the Lord cares for us, providing for our needs and protecting us from enemies.

A great deal of Scripture's poetry is the praise and prayer of the people of God—their deepest feelings about God, life, enemies, fears, hopes, and complaints. Its presence in the Bible teaches us about communicating with God. First, it's okay to express grief, heartache, and even anger to God. Second, it's okay to express displeasure with God's silence or deaf ear, as long as we also acknowledge His sovereignty and care of us. Expressing rage over evil and even desiring the elimination of evil people is also acceptable to Him as long as it is paired with an understanding that we cannot bring justice; He is the judge.

It is impossible to grasp the fullness of a poem's meaning without spending a great deal of time reflecting on its images. God chose to relate the most personal experiences and thoughts of people to us in a literary form that requires reflection to get its full meaning. In order to make the connection between the poem's words and its meaning, we have to meditate on it, slowly chewing it over and over again, savoring the juices of its expression.

Even though many of the Bible's poems are human expressions, God is still the central subject. The psalmists sang their songs to God, praising Him for His greatness. Even in their laments, God was the focus of their worship and the center of their lives.

The Bible as Wisdom Literature

God has also communicated to us through wisdom literature like Job, Proverbs, and Ecclesiastes in the Old Testament, and in the New Testament, the sayings of Jesus as well as the book of James. Wisdom literature is a collection of observations about life written in memorable form. Wise sayings based on observation and experience were passed along in families and communities as guidelines that could be easily remembered. The book of Proverbs illustrates the short, practical, and "memorizable" nature of some wisdom literature.

What do we learn about God from wisdom literature? First, He has given us good heads with the ability to reason and learn—and He expects us to use them. He also expects that we will learn from the past, from the accumulated experiences of others. We do not have to figure everything out for ourselves, but we do need to be smart enough to apply wise principles. Living wisely never guarantees that everything will turn out right, but God has set up the world in such a way that, generally, wise living is rewarded and foolish living is not. In the book of Job, God gives us the exception to this general rule and teaches us that even the most careful living is subject to the sovereignty of God. There is no cause for pride in wise living.

True wisdom, however, is not just careful living and good choices. True wisdom comes from God—"the fear of the Lord is the beginning of knowledge" (Prov 1:7). Our best, most wise choices are those that result from obeying God.

The Bible as Prophetic Literature

God also revealed Himself through prophetic and apocalyptic literature, including sixteen Old Testament books and Revelation in the New

Testament. The more common kind of prophetic writing is "forth-telling," that is, simply proclaiming the Word of God in a particular context and culture. Old Testament prophets, beginning with Moses and continuing through Malachi, were mostly "forth-tellers," carrying out the unwelcome task of standing against the tide, calling the people back to their covenantal agreement with God. The prophets write with intensity and clarity that is not found anywhere else in the Bible, giving us the opportunity to know God in a very personal way. Philip Yancey puts it like this: "Why read the prophets? There is one compelling reason: to get to know God. The prophets are the Bible's most forceful revelation of God's personality."[5]

The prophets were also "fore-tellers," telling of events yet to come. While many of their prophecies had direct application to the people of the day, some also had extended applications to be fulfilled in the future. These fulfillments may have been set for the near future (e.g., the threat of exile in Babylon) or for a more distant future (e.g., the coming of the Messiah). Some prophecies also had multiple fulfillment (e.g., "the virgin will be with child and will give birth to a son" [Isa 7:14] likely referred to a woman in Isaiah's audience [the word for "virgin" can be understood as just a young woman] and it also spoke of Mary hundreds of years later).

Some foretelling literature takes on an "other worldly" sense, incorporating inanimate forces like the sun, moon, stars, and winds and other symbols as actors in God's judgment. This literature is called apocalyptic, and one of its purposes was to jolt readers into looking beyond the real world to see that the cosmos is full of activity relevant to life on earth. God used the visionary literature to show His people that the present might be bad, but the future would be brighter; or He showed them that the present might be good, but it was about to change for the worse. In both of these, God demonstrated His control of history.

God's communication through prophetic writings reveals to us a long-suffering love for disobedient and ungrateful people. He shows His faithfulness in keeping His side of the covenant even when His people disobey, deliberately spurn His love, and serve other gods. God communicates His hatred of sin but His reluctance to inflict punishment; but even then, He reveals that judgment is necessary and ultimately unavoidable.

The Bible as Epistles

Twenty-one out of the twenty-seven books of the New Testament are epistles—letters written by the apostles to first-century believers and churches. These believers were plowing new ground; they knew and believed the

5. Yancey, *The Bible Jesus Read*, 180.

Gospel message, but they needed guidance in developing its implications for church life and personal living. Paul and other early Christian leaders wrote letters to help the believers sort through what it meant to live as followers of Jesus.

These twenty-one letters were not dissertations on systematic theology. Instead they addressed the inquiries of churches (Corinthians), provided encouragement to believers to be strong in difficult times (Hebrews, 1 Peter), and instructed young pastors about caring for young churches (1 and 2 Timothy, Titus). Together these letters provide a mosaic of issues and problems that mirror church life of the first century. Many of these same problems arise today, although they come in different shapes and sizes. God's answers in Scripture are unceasingly relevant. He provides the answers we need to know; if we cannot find the answers we are looking for in the Bible, perhaps we need to ask different questions. He has given us everything we need to know for life and godliness (2 Pet 1:3).

The Bible as Gospels

The four gospels are usually considered to be narratives about the life of Jesus, but really, each is a masterful hodgepodge of genres: biography, genealogy, fiction (i.e., the parables), sermon, speeches, dialogue, proverbs, poetry, tragedy, and even comedy.[6] This combination creates a unique genre not found anywhere else in literature.

The purpose of each gospel is not to give a blow-by-blow account of Jesus' life—far too many details as well as basic facts are omitted for that. Rather, each author used the same collection of events and teachings about Jesus and shaped the material for a particular purpose. For Matthew, writing for a largely Jewish audience, tying Jesus to the Old Testament was important, so he incorporated numerous prophecies to show Jesus as the awaited Messiah. Mark wrote a fast-paced narrative for a Roman audience showing Jesus to be a servant. The detailed historian-physician Luke intended his work for a Greek audience that needed to see Jesus as the perfect Man, while John, the beloved disciple, wrote for all who would believe; he presented Jesus as the Son of God. These generalizations cannot do justice to the wealth and complexity of each gospel, but they at least give a flavor of each gospel's distinctiveness.

What we learn about God in the Gospels is staggering: God Himself came in the flesh in the person of Jesus Christ. The influential people of the day found this communication from God too staggering to accept, and they killed Him—another utterly mind-boggling truth: God Himself

---

6. Ryken, *How to Read the Bible as Literature*, 132.

died in the person of Jesus Christ. And the humanly unbelievable event that happened next can never be explained, only believed by faith: God raised Himself from the dead in the person of Jesus Christ.

God has revealed Himself in time past through writings—poetry, narrative, prophecy, wisdom, even genealogy—but the Gospels proclaim that God also fully revealed Himself through His Son (Heb 1:1–2).

The Bible's Themes

The Bible is a literary masterpiece. God unfolds His purposes through His acts in the lives of people over many centuries of time, and He does so in a Story with a compelling conflict—the struggle between good and evil—where people make choices for or against God and where God is the main character, the one who holds all the events and actions together.

As is true with all good literature, within the single story of the Bible are multiple themes. The dominant theme is the character of God, who He is and what He has done. Another key theme, common to literature, is human experience. The Bible balances its emphasis on the acts of God with an equally strong emphasis on people—their worth, choices, dignity, responsibilities, and importance to God. These two themes usually appear together, comprising the divine-human relationship: "the Bible is a continuous exploration of people's inescapable connections with deity and God's unrelenting interest in what people do."[7]

Human evil and suffering, a result of the disruption in the divine-human relationship, is another theme that involves God's love, His wrath, and the wickedness of people. Biblical authors address how people should behave given their position between sin and virtue, and this behavior "is not pictured as self-exertion toward moral perfection but as submission to God's law or conformity to his character."[8]

Another theme that runs through the Bible is the relation between law and grace (or gospel). "'Law' is anything that exposes human ruin through sin. 'Gospel' refers to everything that displays people's restoration through faith in God's grace."[9] Through the Bible, God makes and fulfills countless promises, providing another theme of great significance.

The Bible is indeed a unique and rich book. Leland Ryken summarizes its magnitude: "Because it is God's purposes that comprise the essential action, the overriding story of the Bible can be called the history of the

---

7. Ibid., 183.
8. Ibid., 184.
9. Ibid., 185.

human race within a providential framework of God's acts of redemption from, and judgment against, the evil in the universe."[10]

God Came—the Word Was Made Flesh

When God spoke at creation, the world came into being. When God "spoke" at the beginning of the new creation, Jesus the Word entered the world He had created. Communication through words lies at the heart of God's plan.

In the person of Jesus, for the first time we glimpse the fullness of God and the fullness of His intentions for the world. God the Son incarnated in flesh and bones revealed God to the people of His day and to everyone else since. Jesus demonstrated God's attitudes, His judgments, and what is important to Him. He, in human flesh like ours, revealed God's heart to us. He showed and told us that God loves sinners, the despised, the outcasts, and the poor. His sacrificial death on the cross as punishment for our sins was the greatest display of love that the world has ever witnessed. What we learn from the fullness of God's revelation is enough to keep us busy for eternity. In this section, we'd like to highlight just a few truths from the incarnation that perhaps you have not considered as fully as others.

The Changing of the Unchangeable God

Every Christmas we appropriately marvel at the wonder of the incarnation. That God became flesh and dwelt among us is an historical fact that ought to never cease amazing us. Because He became one of us, He could be the sacrifice necessary for our salvation; because He became one of us, He is our empathetic high priest—nothing we face is outside His own experience; because He became one of us, we have an ever-present advocate before the Father interceding for us.

Perhaps even more astonishing than each of these facts, however, is that in the incarnation, the unchanging God permanently changed Himself for the sake of redeeming His creation. The Trinity, eternally Father, Son, and Holy Spirit, will always be Father, Son, and Holy Spirit, but now and forevermore, one of the members is also human. God forever altered Himself when the Son took on human flesh and became like us. Jesus will be fully human, wearing skin like ours, forever. More accurately, we will wear skin like His glorified skin forever because He came. Our bodies, apart from the resurrection of Jesus, were destined for dust; after the resurrection of Jesus, however, we rest in the knowledge that someday

---

10. Ibid., 179.

our bodies will be made new, never to decay again, just like Jesus' body. Consider just for a moment how valuable God's creation—all of it—is to Him if He decreed Himself to take on human form and participate bodily in what He made for all eternity.

The God of the Unexpected . . . and Unaccepted

The fullness of God's revelation in Jesus also communicates to us about His way of doing things. While we affirm that God is "high and lifted up," He does not always act like it, and the incarnation is the best illustration of this. The unconventional, even "unacceptable," approach to saving the world seen in the incarnation does not look very "God-like": if we had scripted the events, we would have done them in a way that made God look like *God*, not a squalling, helpless infant in a feeding trough. If we had written the storyline, we would have exalted Jesus for the God He was, not stripped Him naked and scourged Him within an inch or less of His life.

Martin Luther called this the theology of the cross: while we are on our way up to find the exalted God, He passes us on his way down to depths that "God" should never occupy. We have things all turned around; the way to God is not through wisdom, glory, and power, but through suffering, through the cross. The Bible calls this message the foolishness of God (1 Cor 1:18–25), and it cuts against every sense we have of the way things ought to be.

The incarnation shows us that God's ways are not our ways at all, and if we are to be His followers, we must let Him reshape the way we think about everything. Few messages of Christianity are more counter-cultural than this.

The Unreachable God Reaches

A final consideration about the incarnation is that it shows us the nature of God's communication, providing the model for what our communication should be. From creation, there was a distinct division between who God is and who we are—Creator and created. Nonetheless, God created people to communicate intimately with Him. Adam and Eve did so in the garden, before the fall, but the fall changed everything about relationships and communication, beginning with man's relationship to God. Sin put an even greater divide between us and God, a divide that we are incapable of spanning. After sin entered the world, God was unreachable.

As already discussed in this chapter, God communicated to humanity after the fall through the prophets and through His written Word, but those were just shadows of a bridge and not enough to close the gap. It was not until God, through the incarnation, crossed the divide created by sin that we have any way to reach Him at all. He stooped to our level so we could be reached. He became one of us so we could be like Him. He spoke on our level, in words that—through Jesus the Word—we would understand. John Calvin, describing God's communication on our level, compares him to a nurse lisping to young children: "Such modes of expression . . . do not so much express what kind of a being God is, as accommodate the knowledge of him to our feebleness."[11] Lauren Winner puts it this way:

> Here is the thing about God. He is so big and so perfect that we can't really understand Him. We can't possess Him, or apprehend Him. Moses learned this when he climbed up Mount Sinai and saw that the radiance of God's face would burn him up should he gaze upon it directly. But God so wants to be in relationship with us that He makes himself small, smaller than He really is, smaller and more humble than his infinite, perfect self, so that we might be able to get to Him, a little bit.[12]

In the incarnation, God shows us that we must speak to people on their level if they are to understand us and we are to have any relationship with them at all.

Modeled After, but Messed Up

Without a doubt, we are designed after the image of the One who created us to "bubble over," sharing ourselves with others and delighting in them. We reflect a God who has made Himself known to us through His speech, His written Word, and in the flesh. In the very beginning, an awareness of God was clear and uncluttered by sin. Before the fall, Adam and Eve clearly understood God's communication with them—Adam knew what God meant when He told him to tend the garden and name the animals, and the episode in the garden after their sin shows that both Adam and Eve had understood His prohibition about the tree of the knowledge of good and evil. But after the fall all lines of communication were obstructed and corrupted by sin. No longer do God's ways of communicating dominate, but instead, Satan's communication techniques have become

---

11. Calvin, *The Institutes of the Christian Religion*, 110.
12. Winner, *Girl Meets God: On the Path to a Spiritual Life*, 74.

standard operating procedure for humankind—deception, accusation, and destruction.

The Fall—the Beginning of Deceptive, Accusative, and Destructive Communication

It did not take long for God's clear communication with people to be interrupted and obstructed. In Genesis 3, Satan suggests to Eve that God was withholding valuable information; he questioned the goodness and validity of what God had said, and through his words, he raised doubts in Eve's mind. As she listened to Satan's offer of a more glamorous and enlightened future, she began to believe him. By the time the exchange ended, Satan had handed out membership cards to his first recruits. We have been card-carrying members ever since—readily listening to his lies about God, the way the world works, and even ourselves. Not only do we listen and believe *his* lies but we tell quite a few of our own.

When God entered the garden in the cool of the first day of sin, He asked the cowering couple what they had done. He was not seeking information; He was looking for acknowledgement. He was inviting His beloved ones to *confess*—in Greek, the word means "to say the same thing." God invited Adam and Eve to say the same thing about their behavior as He did—that is, that it was sin. But they declined His invitation to accept responsibility for their sin, and instead blamed someone else for it. Adam blamed Eve and Eve blamed the serpent.

What began as an alluring promise proved empty and destructive for Adam and Eve. First, believing the lie of Satan severed the divine-human relationship: Adam and Eve no longer desired God's presence in their midst and they hid from Him. Secondly, in their blame game the couple drove a wedge into their own relationship and those of every human being after them. Instead of truly *commune*-icating, we approach each other with our guards up and our swords drawn. Because of Adam and Eve's sin, our thought patterns revolve around ourselves instead of others, we use sin-tainted language in our communication, and we refuse to take responsibility for our actions. Satan's simple turn of phrase in the garden resulted in the perversion of every human conversation to follow.

This evil pattern of language spiraled into greater forms of destruction. Angry at his brother, Cain used language to lure him to an isolated area where he murdered him. When confronted by God, who again was not looking for information but acknowledgement and confession, Cain used language to deny any knowledge of or responsibility for Abel's death.

This denial of wrongdoing became boasting in Cain's descendent Lamech whose murderous exploits are recorded in his song about his retaliatory killing of a young man who had wounded him (Gen 4:23–24). The spiral reached its lowest depth in Genesis 6:5 where we read these horrible words about humankind: "every inclination of his heart was only evil all the time." What God had intended for good—that is, language—man had corrupted for evil.

The Tower of Babel—the Muddling of Communication (and the Reason for High School Spanish)

Communication patterns became corrupt because of two people's sin, but the rebellion of many people altered the very words of language. Initially, all people on the earth spoke the same language (and it wasn't King James English), and just like He had told Adam and Eve, God instructed Noah and his sons after the flood to fill the earth. But the descendents of Shem, Ham, and Japheth did the exact opposite, clustering and settling together in a very fertile plain known as the Fertile Crescent:

> Now the whole world had one language and common speech. As men moved eastward, they found a plain in Shinar and settled there.
>
> They said to each other, "Come, let us make bricks and bake them thoroughly." They used brick instead of stone, and tar for mortar. Then they said, "Come, let us build ourselves a city, with a tower that reaches to the heavens, so that we may make a name for ourselves and not be scattered over the face of the whole earth."
>
> But the LORD came down to see the city and the tower that the men were building. The LORD said, "If as one people speaking the same language they have begun to do this, then nothing they plan to do will be impossible for them. Come, let us go down and confuse their language so they will not understand each other."
>
> So the LORD scattered them from there over all the earth, and they stopped building the city. That is why it was called Babel—because there the LORD confused the language of the whole world. From there the LORD scattered them over the face of the whole earth. (Gen 11:1–9)

The plan to settle in one area and build a city and tower to "make a name" for themselves was arrogant rebellion against God's clear instructions. God thwarted the arrogant plan by mixing up the language so the people could not understand each other. Few things create greater distance than not being able to communicate, and at Babel, the loss of ability to communicate drove the people apart. As the people scattered, different people groups and cultures developed, each with its distinctive language, thought patterns, and customs.

The Overflow of the Heart—the Real Source of Corrupt Communication

We see evidence of communication's corruption and confusion every day when someone misunderstands us, when we fail to express affection for loved ones, or when we catch news clips from Al Jazeera television. What is impossible to see, however, is where these problems continue to originate. We are nowhere near the garden of Eden or the tower of Babel, yet the corruption and confusion continue unabated because the real source of the corruption lies in the human heart. Each of us effortlessly contributes to the verbal melee because the potential for evil speech is always present in each of us.

In a discussion with the religious leaders of His day, Jesus affirmed this truth: "What comes out of a man is what makes him 'unclean.' For from within, out of men's hearts, come evil thoughts, sexual immorality, theft, murder, adultery, greed, malice, deceit, lewdness, envy, slander, arrogance and folly. All these evils come from inside and make a man 'unclean'" (Mark 7:20–23). Words and deeds proceed from our thought life, a life known only to each of us personally and to God.

The Apostle Paul enlarges upon the words of Jesus: "They have become filled with every kind of wickedness, evil, greed and depravity. They are full of envy, murder, strife, deceit and malice. They are gossipers, slanderers, God-haters, insolent, arrogant and boastful; they invent ways of doing evil; they disobey parents; they are senseless, faithless, heartless, ruthless" (Rom 1:29–31). This description may not fit most of us completely, but it does reveal the potential of every human heart.

Modeled After, Messed Up, and Made New

Although corrupted by sin, God's amazing gift of language is not out of redemption's reach. Followers of Jesus Christ as the redeemed image of God are called and equipped to use speech in clear, appropriate, and worthwhile ways—a sharp contrast to the deceptive, accusatory, and destructive patterns established by sin. James assures us that this is not an easy task, but it is nonetheless one that can set believers apart from unbelievers.

Redeemed patterns of language begin with the sober recognition that communicative ability is a God-given ability to be treasured and used as a sacred trust, something of great value to be used for the glory of God.

When Wendy shared a Christian college dorm bathroom with approximately twenty Christian women, someone decided to hang "chat sheets" inside the stall doors—study break entertainment, we suppose. All sorts of worthless graffiti made its way onto the sheets; crude jokes and campus gossip invited the young women to contribute their own comments to the wall. In an attempt to raise the quality of communication, Wendy and her roommate replaced the chat sheets with fresh papers headed by verses about edifying and worthwhile speech, hoping their hall would use words to build up rather than tear down. They were disheartened instead to find scribbles bordering on blasphemy below the sacred words of God. They quickly removed the new sheets, and the only good result was that no one put the old ones back up.

The truth is that we do not own our mouths. Every part of us has been bought at a very high price—the life of the very Word of God; we bear His mark and have been commissioned to be His voice wherever we go.

Our words are powerful, capable of great harm. Consider Pharaoh's "no" to Moses and Aaron. Consider Peter's "I don't know Him!" around the campfire before Jesus' trial. Consider the words, "You're fat" to an adolescent girl. Consider the judge's verdict of "guilty" to a defendant.

James calls the tongue "a fire, a world of evil among the parts of the body. It corrupts the whole person, sets the whole course of his life on fire, and is itself set on fire by hell" (3:6). This small member wields more power and is infinitely harder to control than a clenched fist: "All kinds of animals, birds, reptiles and creatures of the sea are being tamed and have been tamed by man, but no man can tame the tongue. It is a restless evil, full of deadly poison" (Jas 3:7–8). Yet, as the redeemed image of God, we must take action to control it; the overflow of our changed hearts should be changed language.

The Bible includes a litany of potential "verbal violations" to be avoided. Just a sampling includes slander, false testimony, and unwholesome talk:

- "Brothers, do not slander one another. Anyone who speaks against his brother or judges him speaks against the law and judges it." (Jas 4:11)
- "You shall not give false testimony against your neighbor." (Exod 20:16)
- "Do not let any unwholesome talk come out of your mouths, but only what is helpful for building others up according to their needs, that it may benefit those who listen. Get rid of all bitterness, rage and anger, brawling and slander, along with every form of malice." (Eph 4:29, 31)

But if words have the potential for destruction, they have just as much—or more—power for good. Consider God's "Let there be light!" on the first day of creation. Consider Paul's "Believe on the Lord Jesus Christ and you will be saved!" to the Philippian jailer. Consider the smiling father's "Wow!" at his daughter's report card. Consider the "Stop" on the sign at a busy intersection.

Not surprisingly, the Bible provides some clues for controlling our tongues, beginning with James's admonition to "be quick to listen, slow to speak and slow to become angry" (Jas 1:19–20). A sample of the rest includes encouraging, thanking, and being gracious:

- "Let the word of Christ dwell in you richly as you teach and admonish one another with all wisdom, and as you sing psalms, hymns and spiritual songs with gratitude in your hearts to God. And whatever you do, whether in word or deed, do it all in the name of the Lord Jesus, giving thanks to God the Father through him." (Col 3:16–17)
- "Be joyful always; pray continually; give thanks in all circumstances, for this is God's will for you in Christ Jesus." (1 Thess 5:16–18)
- "Be wise in the way you act toward outsiders; make the most of every opportunity. Let your conversation be always full of grace, seasoned with salt, so that you may know how to answer everyone." (Col 4:5–6)

As the verses above and many others like them demonstrate, controlling the tongue depends on heart attitudes. Changed hearts will result in changed speech patterns. We are the redeemed people of God whose speech should be gracious and appropriate for each occasion. The urgency of this cannot be overstated since others, for better or worse, judge us by the words we say.

Communication and School Subjects

Language arts comprise the school subjects that intersect most directly with communication: reading, spelling, grammar, composition, creative writing, penmanship, speech, and foreign languages. The collective goal of language arts is to teach students to be good senders and receivers: to be able to say something worthwhile in a clear and appropriate way, and to be able to receive the expressions of others with attentive respect.

Communication

Writing—Putting the "Overflow of Our Hearts" on Paper

The ability to write is an essential part of life in the West, whether it's as simple as keeping a shopping list or as complex as writing a doctoral dissertation or a multimillion dollar grant proposal. Some writing clearly showcases the overflow of the heart: personal letters, notes of encouragement, Sunday school lessons, or song lyrics. While other kinds of writing, such as answers on a pop quiz, "to do" lists, or applications for a checking account, may not seem to overtly show the heart, they are nonetheless influenced by the attitudes and values we have. The importance of writing cannot be overestimated by Christian educators. We teach the alphabet in order to write words in order to construct sentences in order to compose paragraphs, and we teach penmanship and keyboarding so the paragraphs are legible! All these subjects work together to provide effective ways to express the overflow of the heart.

Reading—Discovering the Familiar and the Unfamiliar on Paper

Reading can take us places we will never go, introduce us to people we will never meet in person, and carry us through adventures we will otherwise never experience—all from the comforts of the living room recliner. Literature, an especially rich kind of reading experience, takes us deep into the head and heart of the human race and helps humanize us by fostering awareness of ourselves and the world: "It enlarges our compassion for people. It awakens our imaginations. It expresses our feelings and insights about God, nature, and life. It enlivens our sense of beauty. And it is a constructive form of entertainment."[13] In short, reading of all genres allows us to understand God's multi-faceted world with just a turn of the page.

Reading goes hand-in-hand with writing—unless something has been written, it cannot be read. Sounds obvious enough, but the implications of this are two-fold. First, because writing expresses the overflow of the heart, nothing written is entirely "objective" or "neutral," even if it claims to be. Second, then, good reading requires discernment, recognizing the worldviews of the writers and critically evaluating the value of their words.

Speech—Moving from the Printed Page to the Whites of Eyes

The ease with which most of us speak evaporates when we have to stand and speak to an audience: our palms sweat, hearts race, knees knock, and in extreme cases, our bodies even collapse. Given this prevailing human

---

13. Ryken, *Windows to the World: Literature in Christian Perspective*, 34.

tendency, why do teachers inflict what could be considered torture in the form of oral book reports, poetry recitations, and formal speeches?

While most of our students will not be famous orators or highly public figures, the vast majority of them will encounter situations where the only way people will know their thoughts is if they stand up and express them . . . without fainting. Good communication begins with having worthwhile thoughts, but it is completed by those who have also practiced the art of expressing thoughts aloud. Because public speaking puts us face to face with our "receivers," it also puts us in positions of great vulnerability; the instant, visible effect of our words could be disbelief, laughter, or boredom—all potentially devastating responses. We miss the mark in teaching public speaking if we only address the *speakers*; we must also teach our students to be good receivers, encouraging others to speak and then listening attentively and graciously to their words. God's image ought to be evidenced in how we speak *and* how we listen.

Foreign Languages—Hearing the Rest of the World and Better Understanding Our Own

Look at any world map made before the onslaught of multiculturalism and observe which country has the central spot in the world. Mapmakers aren't the only ones who put themselves in the place of prominence—we all do, Americans and otherwise. Americans, in particular, however, have developed a worldwide reputation for egocentrism (hence the travel warning against being "ugly Americans"). Generally speaking, we are limited in our knowledge of and appreciation for other cultures. We are not talking about politically correct tolerance; we are talking about, as we discussed extensively in the previous chapter, appreciating and valuing the diversity of people God has created. Thanks to the Internet, today's youth are much more "world savvy" than we ever were, but even these global citizens have sin natures that make them most interested in themselves and frequently prejudiced against others.

Perhaps more than any other school subject, foreign languages create an environment for our students to acquire these traits. Slaving through the verb conjugations and vocabulary lists of a language that does not rest right on the ears is excellent practice for enjoying and appreciating the breadth of God's creativity demonstrated in people and cultures. And strangely enough, the more students learn about different cultures and languages, the more similarities they will find between people groups, and the better understanding they will have of the image of God scattered across the globe.

Conclusion

Communication and being human are inseparable, and human sinfulness affects every kind of communication for every person—short-term and long-term relationships; written works and spoken words; casual conversation and intimate talk. Foreign relations, legislative relations and actions, law enforcement and adherence, parent-child, employer-employee relations are all infected by irresponsible and dishonest communication.

The ability to express oneself is indeed a sacred trust, and the goal of every Christian ought to be to carefully steward this trust. The role of Christian educators is two-fold: influence the heart from which the overflow comes, and give students the tools they need to connect more effectively, to understand more thoroughly, to share more meaningfully.

Finally, as Christians we have one other significant motivation for gaining a certain mastery of words: words are incredibly important to God. It is, in fact, impossible to appreciate God's *works* without contemplating the role of *words* in them. Through both the words of Scripture and the living Word, Jesus, God reaches us. If we want to understand, know, and love Him, we need to be able to accept His words, on His terms.

Summary of Truths

God Is a Communicator

1. He has spoken.
    a. By His words, He created.
    b. He spoke with humans from the very beginning.
    c. Adam and Eve understood what God said.
2. He has written.
    a. The Bible is unique, written by God the Holy Spirit in tandem with human authors.
    b. Each author, directed by God, worked independently, yet contributed to the overall theme and structure of the Bible.
    c. God transmitted His Word to us in the various literary genres of the writers' times.
        i. Narratives recount events in which God interacted with His and other people, and every smaller narrative fits into

the theme of the larger Story. Narratives help us identify with people's experiences, making it easier to understand the Truth being communicated.
- ii. Poetry appeals to our imaginations, requiring us to meditate and ponder to appreciate and understand the fullness of the Truth.
- iii. Psalms are praises and prayers of people to God, and from them we learn that God wants to hear everything that concerns us.
- iv. Prophetic books spoke to the culture of their times, either of judgment or redemption, but some prophecies also spoke of events to come beyond the time of the prophets. A special kind of prophetic literature is apocalyptic, meant to jolt the audience into realizing that there are significant unseen cosmic activities happening continually.
- v. The Gospels are narratives of Jesus Christ, God the Son; each presents a distinctive portrait of Jesus and reveals to us what is important to God.
- vi. The Epistles are letters written by the apostles to churches and individuals to instruct, encourage, and answer questions about issues that are still pertinent today. They are letters, not theological treatises, forcing us to become familiar with the larger context of Scripture so we know how to understand them.

3. He came to us.
   a. Jesus reveals the fullness of God to us in human form.
   b. Through the incarnation, the Trinity forever changed: Jesus will be human, "one of us," forever.
   c. The incarnation shows us how God carries out His plan -- often in ways we might label "unacceptable" ways for God to act.
   d. The incarnation shows the depth to which God was willing to go to reach us. He spoke in our language in a way we could understand.

The "Image of God" in Us

1. Our ability to communicate is a significant aspect of bearing the image of God.

2. The image of God is marred in us, and this shows in the ways we communicate.
    a. Because of the sin of Adam and Eve, we use deceptive, accusative, and destructive communication.
    b. Because of human rebellion at the tower of Babel, the world has many languages.
    c. Because of our own sinfulness, our communication is corrupt. Speech is the overflow of the heart: what we are like inside comes out of our mouths.
3. Language is not out of the reach of redemption.
    a. The Christian believer is faced with the need (and the ability) to use speech in a way that reveals the new nature.
    b. The Christian, made in God's likeness, is to use speech in a way that will represent God well.

Communication and School

1. Schooling helps children develop their God-endowed communication ability to become good senders and receivers.
2. Reading helps us learn about and communicate with others in the world around us.
    a. Every author writes from the perspective of a worldview.
    b. When Christians read, they need to identify the worldviews at work. This will make them critical and discriminating learners.
3. Writing enables children to communicate "the overflow of the heart" in written form throughout their lives.
4. Proficiency in reading and writing will allow children to learn the maximum about God's created natural world and develop a greater appreciation of Him.
5. Public speaking includes learning how to speak well in front of people, as well as how to listen well to others.
6. Studying foreign languages helps students better appreciate the world and it can help put their own culture in perspective.

Teaching Tips

1. A Place Fit for the King. Brainstorm with elementary students about how God should appear in the world. Don't preface your discussion

with any notion of what Jesus did and be sure to avoid "showing your hand" so they do not know where you're headed. Draw out from them how we might script the presence of someone as important as God in the world. Where should He live; what should His house look like; what kind of car might He drive; how would you approach His house; etc. Have them draw pictures creating what they think God's life would be like if He lived in your city. Display the pictures on the board or on a bulletin board, and sing some praise songs about how great God is. Do multiple things to drive home the point (without saying it) of how things "should have been" with God in the world—His living conditions as well as the treatment He should have received from people. Again, be careful not to show your hand throughout this or the shock value of the "theology of the cross" will be lost.

For driving home the point, you need to find several pictures or video clips of life in the lowest places of *our* culture: a homeless person, a food pantry, a prison. Still, be careful not to show your hand, and ask your students as you show them pictures, "Would this be God?" or "Would we put God here?" or "Would we find God in a place like this?" Then make your point—that's *exactly* where we find God in the person of Jesus. Discuss what it meant for Jesus to live the way He did. Put your pictures over the "ideal pictures" drawn by your students and also put a large cross in the center of the picture board. (Elementary grades)

2. Biblical Literature. Have students interact with each genre of the Bible referenced in this chapter: select texts from Scripture and work through them from a literary perspective, noting the incredible quality of the written words of God; have students produce forms in the same genres. Identify ways we might read texts incorrectly by "misreading" the genre (for example, reading prophetic metaphors literally or reading wisdom literature as covenantal promises). Have fun with genre and getting to know the Bible as a literary work. (Junior high and high school)

3. It's, Like, a Proverb. Use Proverbs and other similar verses to teach simile and metaphor. Have each student or small group select a proverb and make a poster of the "literal" meaning of the simile/metaphor. On their poster have them include a paragraph explaining what the proverb means or have them write a story that illustrates (1) the proverb at work, (2) how the proverb might have been developed based on

observations of life, or (3) the foolish behavior explicit or implicit in the proverb. (Upper elementary and higher)

4. Create and Recreate. Do a literary comparison of the original creation account and John's account of the beginning of the "new creation" in John 1 by putting Genesis 1 and John 1 side by side. You can also draw in Revelation 21–22 to expand the comparison further. (High school)

5. Standing on Their Shoulders. Each generation adds to the learning of previous generations (we "stand on their shoulders"), and it is important for our students to appreciate the history that leads to present-day disciplines. Compile a list of Christians who have worked in your subject area, and as part of your semester's assigned workload, have students read a biography of a Christian in your field and report in writing or to the class what the person accomplished, how faith influenced his or her studies, and what legacy he or she has left. (Junior high and high school)

Additional Resources[14]

1. Andrews, Adam. *Teaching the Classics*. Atascadero, CA: Institute for Excellence in Writing/Center for Literary Education. A DVD training course, this material provides instruction about the basics of literary interpretation and analysis, using the Socratic question/answer method. For use with all ages, it includes a comprehensive list of questions that can be customized for any book. www.writing-edu.com.

2. Cowen, Louise, and Os Guiness, eds. *Invitation to the Classics: A Guide to Books You've Always Wanted to Read*. Grand Rapids: Baker Books, 1998. Providing an analysis of seventy-five enduring books of Western culture from a Christian worldview, this guide invites readers to learn more about the great authors and books of the West.

3. Fee, Gordon D., and Douglas Stuart. *How to Read the Bible for All Its Worth*. Grand Rapids: Zondervan, 1981, 1993. This is a guide to biblical interpretation for everything, whether a beginning Bible reader, an experienced one, or one somewhere in between. It provides a practical approach to Bible study—one that both makes sense and is easy to understand. Included is a list of recommended commentaries and resources.

---

14. Thanks to Danielle Olander for her help in compiling this list of resources.

4. Hunt, Gladys. *Honey for a Child's Heart.* 4th ed. Grand Rapids: Zondervan, 2002. This classic book is a wonderful publication on the value of reading, especially for children. Included is an annotated list of books for ages 0–12.

5. Pudawa, Andrew. *Teaching Writing with Structure and Style.* Atascadero, CA: Institute for Excellence in Writing. This is a DVD training course that shows teachers how to teach writing using history, science, and literature. By encouraging writing about subject areas, this method reinforces knowledge and gives relevance for writing. To obtain materials from the Institute for Excellence in Writing, visit: www.writing-edu.com.

6. Ryken, Leland. *Windows to the World: Literature in Christian Perspective.* Eugene, OR: Wipf and Stock, 2000. Ryken has several titles that deal with a biblical approach to literature and imagination. This particular book offers helpful information about the rights and responsibilities of Christian readers.

7. Ryken, Leland, ed. *The Christian Imagination: The Practice of Faith in Literature and Writing.* Colorado Springs: Shaw Books, 2002. This compilation includes essays and excerpts from fifty authors such as J. R. R. Tolkien, Madeleine L'Engle, C. S. Lewis, and Flannery O'Connor, and addresses how to think "Christianly about literature."

8. Schultze, Quentin J. *Communicating for Life: Christian Stewardship in Community and Media.* Grand Rapids: Baker Books, 2000. Offering a holistic Christian view of communication in this discerning introduction to communication theory, Schultze takes his readers through an interesting and creative study of communication, a highly religious activity.

9. Whitworth, Lou. "Literature and the Christian Imagination: What is literature, and what is its purpose?" Whitworth's article on the website of Probe Ministries provides a wonderful list of resources at the end of the page: http://www.northave.org/MGManual/Literature/Lit3.htm

4
Beauty

> 'Twas the night of the program, and all through the halls,
> the children were making their teachers climb walls.
> Their stocking-clad feet would not be kept still.
> They vaulted, they leapt, they danced fit to kill . . .
>
> Somehow the show happened, in spite of the crew—
> the small, active children, with great things to do.
> Their eyes, how they twinkled, and how they did squint.
> To headaches they'd started, they gave not a hint!
> They spoke not a word, but faced straight ahead.
> Their cherubic faces were flushed with bright red.
> And backstage the teachers caught snickers and pokes,
> While those in the audience ate up the jokes.
> They loved it, adored it; they clapped long and loud,
> not knowing what happened to ensure they were wowed . . .[1]

The annual Christmas extravaganza at our Christian school gets rave reviews from parents, grandparents, and friends who attend. The sight and sound of five hundred energetic children dressed in every color of the rainbow, singing, swaying, and performing is a sight to behold. For the teachers, backstage is also a sight to behold, and it's only the composite beauty of the final product that makes their Excedrin-sized headaches worth it.

Beauty in process is messy, seldom reflective of the final product. Few places showcase this as well as elementary school and its screech of third-grade flutophones, ear assaults of fifth-grade band concerts, finger-painted masterpieces (on the easel and on the floor), inaudible mumbles of memorized poems, mismatched outfits of strong-willed seven-year-olds, and indecipherable cursive of left-handed boys.

While the three *R*s form the core of our academic curriculum, the arts provide the components that shape the soul. We certainly want our students to be able to function in the world, using their cognitive skills in fields of math and science, business and politics, education and journalism, but we also want those cognitive skills to be drenched with creativity,

---

1. Widder, "'Twas the Night of the Program," 16.

beauty, and freshness—not mere function. We want our students to enjoy the world and their part in it "just because"—just because God made it a beautiful place for no apparent reason other than our enjoyment and His glory. Bottom lines, progress, and success may have their place, but they are only part of a much larger picture.

Teachers know their students will not excel at everything, but nonetheless, we make them try everything because appreciation for and ability to produce beauty are, for the most part, learned skills. Most of us have to learn the hard way how to do the things we will eventually excel in: virtuoso musicians rehearsed, champion athletes practiced, five-star chefs experimented. We cannot speak and create beauty as God did; our reflection of Him in this area happens as we develop our interests and hone our skills. In school, we provide students with opportunities to discover the ways beauty can flow from their fingertips, and we hope for graduates who will make beautiful homes, workplaces, churches, and communities.

Beauty is taught in dozens of ways—through the formal instruction of art class or music lessons, the rhythmic reading of a well-crafted story, a field trip to the local children's theater, playing classical music during study hall, and analyzing the techniques of Shakespeare. Our budding musicians, artists, authors, public speakers, homemakers, seamstresses, architects, and designers are sponges, and the more we expose them to beauty and encourage their development of it, the greater their appreciation and skills will be.

God has delighted in sharing His beauty with us, but He also enjoys the beauty we create. The world is more than functional, and as our students advance in the "curriculum of beauty," we pray they better appreciate and love the Master of it.

Introduction

> Great is the LORD, and most worthy of praise,
>   in the city of our God, his holy mountain.
> It is beautiful in its loftiness,
>   the joy of the whole earth. (Ps 48:1–2)
>
> Your beauty should not come from outward adornment...
> Instead, it should be that of your inner self,
> the unfading beauty of a gentle and quiet spirit,
> which is of great worth in God's sight. (1 Pet 3:3–4)

PRISTINE MOUNTAIN waters shimmer far from human eyes. Wildflowers grow unbidden on forgotten trails. Cotton clouds drift across an azure backdrop on a sun-soaked day, and hours later, the glowing sun drops below the horizon in a brilliant display of fiery color. God did not merely make a functional world; He made an incredibly beautiful one. He put beauty in out-of-the-way places, a reflection of His care for every detail and a reminder that the greatest treasures of beauty are enjoyed only by those who take the time to observe them.

We all care about beauty to some degree, and we each have our own way of expressing it: a neighbor washes his convertible every weekend, a gardener carefully arranges her flowerbeds, the woodworker selects just the right shade of stain. When no one is looking or forcing us to make decisions, we work hard to get every detail, nuance, and jot and tittle just right—not because anyone will notice, but simply for the sake of it. And in the process of cultivating beauty for its own sake, we reflect the One who gave nothing less than the same kind of attention to every aspect of creation.

What is beauty? Beauty, as a part of the larger philosophical discipline of aesthetics, is the internal quality of a thing or person that provides pleasure to the senses and the mind. Because we image God, we all have the ability to appreciate and create beautiful things. God also equipped us with five senses for receiving images of beauty. The more senses we use to soak in an experience, the more intense the pleasure will be: the fragrance of a flower draws us close enough to see and touch the petals and to admire their design and texture, enhancing our appreciation of its beauty.

In this chapter we will first explore the beauty God created for our enjoyment, and then we will consider His inherent beauty. We will also look at beauty that we create by using God's raw materials. Finally we will consider how our imaginations and senses work together to shape our unique appreciations of beauty.

God's Beauty

The Beauty of God in What He Made

The author of beauty is God. All you have to do is look up at the night sky, gaze across a field of wildflowers, or peer up at snowcapped mountains to realize this. While God was creating the initial beauty of our planet, He stamped His approval on it six times: "God saw that it was good" (Gen 1:4, 10, 12, 18, 21, 25). It was not only good in a useful sense; it was good in its appearance. It was full of beauty.

God's Greenhouse

> Then God said, "Let the land produce vegetation: seed-bearing plants and trees on the land that bear fruit with seed in it, according to their various kinds." And it was so. The land produced vegetation: plants bearing seed according to their kinds and trees bearing fruit with seed in it according to their kinds. And God saw that it was good. (Gen 1:11–12)

Our planet is carpeted with grass, decorated with flowers, and bulging with fruit. The fragrances, colors, shapes, and sizes that comprise Earth's plant life overwhelm the senses. Beauty is everywhere—even in weeds![2] The beauty of plant life is seen in its function and its form: branches give a plant its shape, while the leaves grow on those branches and stems in such a way as to gain maximum exposure to sunlight. Fruit-bearing plants produce edible food filled with vital nutrients, yet each plant has unique blossoms, colors, and fruit.

Many green plants that do not produce edible fruit nonetheless produce food for the eyes: flowers. Careful planning at our Midwestern home provides a parade of flowers throughout the spring and summer. April welcomes snowdrops, crocuses, and daffodils, and May brings lilacs, peonies, irises, tulips, and even dandelions; June displays more peonies and irises, poppies, clematises, lupines; July features day lilies, phlox, daisies, and rose of Sharon. During the dog days of August hibiscus and black-eyed Susans color the terrain, then before the splash of fall leaves and the first frost, we enjoy fall crocuses and an autumn clematis. And when the landscape loses its color, we appreciate even more our houseplants, poinsettias, cut flowers, and Easter lilies.

While all plants are similar in many ways, each green plant is slightly different in its stem, flower, seeds, or leaves. Some prefer shade, others sun; some like it hot and some like it cold; some dry, others wet. The variety in plants is even more amazing when we realize that we cannot produce a single original plant or flower. We can tinker with the genetic structure of a species to develop new varieties, frequently hybrids, but many of these varieties cannot reproduce themselves. Beauty originates with God; we are imitators.

---

2. Did you ever wonder why God bothered to make weeds beautiful? The fact that weeds—a byproduct of the fall—can be beautiful is a startling testimony to God's appreciation for beauty.

God's Animal Farm

> And God said, "Let the water teem with living creatures, and let birds fly above the earth across the expanse of the sky". . . And God said, "Let the land produce living creatures according to their kinds: livestock, creatures that move along the ground, and wild animals, each according to its kind." And it was so. (Gen 1:20, 24)

In chapter one we considered the variety of creatures God made—thousands of species of birds, fish, insects, and countless other animals. There is a creature for every personality, and each one is a masterpiece of utility and beauty.

Some creatures, like the delicate butterflies that flit through our flowerbeds, invite our admiration because of their appearance. Others, like the songbirds that dine at our backyard feeders, we enjoy for the sounds they make. Still others, like kittens cuddled in our arms, we appreciate for their soft-to-the-touch feel. And some even have their "beauty" appreciated most in a tender grilled steak. God created a feast for the senses when He designed the world's zoo.

The beauty of animals is in their variety, and while scientists can provide explanations for many of the unique features of animals—like the snout of the anteater, the skin of an alligator, and the translucent fur on a polar bear—the fact is that God did not *have* to design each of these creatures in the way He did. We wouldn't be surprised if He intentionally painted an extra stroke of color on the toucan, deliberated a few seconds longer on the penguin's waddle, stuffed some extra fluff in the llama's coat, and even laughed at the platypus. He created a worldwide zoo that showcases His delight in detail and His concern with beauty.

God's Terrarium and Aquarium

> And God said, "Let the water under the sky be gathered to one place, and let the dry ground appear." And it was so. God called the dry ground "land," and the gathered waters he called "seas." And God saw that it was good. (Gen 1:9–10)

Nothing in the world is grander than a pile of rock, soil, and vegetation reaching into the skies. Aside from the natural resources provided by mountains, they are there for us to enjoy. The rocky cliffs soaring to the snowcapped peaks, the noisy streams rushing down their sides, and the grass-covered slopes and forests up to the tree line are playgrounds for the most adventurous among us. For campers, climbers, fishermen, and skiers, there is no place like the mountains. Human ingenuity and enterprise cannot duplicate the grandeur and beauty of mountains.

But the planet's flatlands have a beauty of their own as well. The great plains of the United States, the steppes of Russia, the pampas of Argentina, and the prairie provinces of Canada provide grazing for cattle and fertile soil for food crops. The hundreds of thousands of acres of fertile soil with their stalks of grain swaying in the wind are oceans of golden waves.

Surrounding these landforms are oceans and dotted across them are freshwater lakes and rivers. Nearly three-fourths of the earth's surface is covered with water, and in these waters teem every color, shape, and size of fish imaginable. The water provides a favorite getaway for people. Some of us like to sit on a riverbank and fish, while others of us like to lie on our backs under a tree in a quiet wooded area and listen to a brook babble. Lakes are perfect for swimming, water skiing, jet skiing, fishing, sailing, or just sitting in a beach chair being lulled to sleep by the lap of the waves.

The earth's landforms and bodies of water arouse our sense of awe and wonder. They are natural wonders designed by God for our use but also for our enjoyment.

God's Planetarium

> The heavens declare the glory of God;
>   the skies proclaim the work of his hands.
> Day after day they pour forth speech;
>   night after night they display knowledge. (Ps 19:1–2)

The sky is a continuous display of the vastness of the universe. The faithful sun sends light and heat every day, and at night it reflects a softer version of its light off the moon to dispel a little of the darkness. The stars seem numberless and randomly strewn across the sky, but they are neither; God knows how many there are—even when some fall!—and He set them in assigned places. The North Star is always in its place, and the constellations fall in their places.

On a bright and sunny day clouds may fill the sky; sometimes large billowy puffy white clouds and other days high wispy clouds. Other times dark ominous clouds punctuated with thunder and lightning descend, a dazzling display of power followed by the gentle beauty of a rainbow, a reminder of God's covenant with Noah never to destroy the earth with a flood again (Gen 9:8–17).

On clear mornings and evenings, the sky is painted with the colors of a rising or setting sun, and no matter how many times we see the show, each has its unique beauty. The best place to watch sunrises and sunsets is near a lake where the foreground provides a double show for the price of one with the reflection of the sunset on the surface of the water.

God's beauty is reflected all around us in creation. He has made a universe marked with intricate detail and fathomless variety; we cannot escape seeing Him unless we close our eyes and our minds to His clear revelation. But His beauty is evident beyond the works of His hands. We see beauty in God's person, who He is.

The Beauty of God in Who He Is

> One thing I ask of the Lord,
>   this is what I seek:
> that I may dwell in the house of the Lord
>   all the days of my life,
> to gaze upon the beauty of the Lord
>   and to seek him in his temple. (Ps 27:4)

The beauty of God, a theme that flows through the Scriptures from Genesis to Revelation, is expressed most often by the word *glory*, but also by *splendor*, *majesty*, *beautiful*, and *greatness*. God is glorious in His very person: His holiness, His love and mercy, His longsuffering, His joy—just a handful of His attributes that reflect His beauty. All of these attributes (also called perfections) together enable us to know Him. The ones listed here and detailed below relate particularly to our personal relationship with Him.

God is beautiful in His holiness. He is the only Being not flawed by sin. When the disciples see Jesus transfigured before them and they glimpse the holiness of God, they are stunned and afraid because of His magnificence. When John sees Jesus in Revelation, he falls on his face. When Isaiah encounters God in the temple, he cries, "I am ruined!" (Isa 6:5). When Ezekiel beholds the throne of God, he sits stunned and silent for seven days. A common thread weaves its way through the Bible's stories of people confronted with the holiness of God: they are afraid because seeing God's holiness reminds us of our unholiness and our unworthiness to be in His presence. But this holiness is nonetheless beautiful. The Bible pictures holiness by whiteness: "Though your sins are like scarlet, they shall be as white as snow" (Isa 1:18); "As I looked, thrones were set in place, and the Ancient of Days took his seat. His clothing was as white as snow" (Dan 7:9); "There he was transfigured before them. His clothes became dazzling white, whiter than anyone in the world could bleach them" (Mark 9:2–3);

"His clothes became as bright as a flash of lightning" (Luke 9:29). God's holiness is beautiful because in it lies our hope to be holy as well: "Be holy, because I am holy" (1 Pet 1:16). We can be holy because of what God, in His holiness, has done for us in Jesus.

God is beautiful in His love and mercy, seen most clearly in His redemptive acts on our behalf. Paul says in Romans 5:6–8, "You see, at just the right time, when we were still powerless, Christ died for the ungodly. Very rarely will anyone die for a righteous man, though for a good man someone might possibly dare to die. But God demonstrates his love for us in this: While we were still sinners, Christ died for us." To even begin to fathom the greatness of Christ's sacrificial death, we must set Romans 1:18–32 (which describes the depravity of the human heart) alongside this text. Because of our sin, we deserve only God's wrath and destruction, but His mercy caused Him to look past our sinful hearts and extend His love to us, as undeserved as it was. Few of us would look past the evil deeds and heart of a convicted child molester and killer and extend love and forgiveness to him; we have a hard time looking past the evil deeds of those who do much less than this. We hold grudges, we seek revenge, we look to advance ourselves. Yet God looks past all our sins and offers forgiveness.

God is beautiful in His longsuffering. Human sin demands punishment, but God delays punishment, extending instead the promise of eternal life with Him. He waits for more people to repent: "The Lord is not slow in keeping his promise, as some understand slowness. He is patient with you, not wanting anyone to perish, but everyone to come to repentance" (2 Pet 3:9). The promise is there for those who forsake their sinful ways and turn to Him in repentance and faith. Just as He waited and accepted a repentant Israel back after they disobeyed Him and turned to false gods, God waits for us today. The verse repeated most often in the Bible first appears in Exodus 34, not long after the Israelites made the golden calf and God threatened their utter destruction. Moses interceded for the sinful people and God responded by sparing them and offering this statement on His character: "The Lord, the Lord God, compassionate and gracious, slow to anger, and abounding in lovingkindness and truth; who keeps lovingkindness for thousands, who forgives iniquity, transgression and sin . . ." (Exod 34:6–7). This precious and beautiful promise is still true.

God is beautiful in His joy. Joy is not the product of pleasant circumstances, but rather an outpouring of inner character. God's joy over us is especially evident in three parables Jesus tells in Luke 15: the lost sheep, the lost coin, and the lost son. In the first two, there is great rejoicing when the owners find their sheep and coin. Jesus adds that there was great joy in heaven over the recovery of the lost items. In the third parable He gives a wonderful picture of the joy of God the Father over each sinner that repents. When the prodigal returned home, his watching father ran to meet him, hugged and kissed him, gave him new clothes, and celebrated with a feast. So God the Father welcomes repentant sinners with great joy. He is not just happy; He is ecstatic. His heart of love overflows with uncontainable joy. We get a taste of this joy right now, but we will enjoy its fullness in His presence forever.

> The living God is majestic and glorious. He is awesome and impressive in his character, nature, tri-unity and works. Whether revealed in the Scriptures or in his creation, his majesty drives honest readers to their knees. The brilliance of the noonday sun, the beauty of a rainbow, the vast numbers of galaxies, the amazing complexity of the atom all remind us of the vastly superior greatness of the God who created and sustains them.
>
> God is beautiful. It is hard for us to recognize this because we have trivialized beauty. But God made us to behold beauty and to delight in it. All of the beauty of things is a reflection of the beauty of God. His beauty is too great and too intense for us to see by looking directly at him. We would be destroyed if we did for no one can see God and live.
>
> But he bends down to show us that perfect, glorious and majestic beauty reflected in his creatures. The beauty of a star-filled sky, a sunrise or sunset, a rainbow, a tiger, a peacock, a child's smile are all little pictures of the edges of his beauty. When we look at them with delight, we should be reminded of him and delighted to know that we will behold that kind of beauty in billions of different ways in the ages to come without ever even beginning to exhaust the wonders of his beauty. He is beautiful and the source of all beauty.[3]

The beauty of who God is invites a response from His creation. Our first response ought to be worship, and our second response is to recognize that as God is beautiful, so we are created and called to radiate beauty to others. Though His image in us is distorted, it is not gone. We can extend love and mercy to others; we can be longsuffering; we can shower joy on those around us; we can live our lives in obedience to His commands and be holy, set apart for Him.

---

3. Crawford, "Systematic Theology 1," 531.

The Beauty of God In Who We Are

Created in the image of God, we are equipped to both enjoy beauty and produce it. God made us with an array of senses to soak in the marvels of His creation, and He instilled in us the imagination and variety of artistic abilities with which to create beauty of our own.

The Senses

God has equipped our bodies with sense organs that send information, stimuli from without and within the body, to our brains. Properly functioning sense organs and receptors give us an awareness of our environment and its many stimuli at all times.

Our sensory receptors include those found in the skin and its deeper tissues, permitting us to sense touch, pressure, temperature, and pain; it also includes the highly complex, intricately designed sense organs that give us sight, hearing, smell, taste, and balance. Because of these, we are able to experience both God's creative works and those of people.

Our five senses work in cooperation so we can continually experience our surroundings. Each sense is very complex and intricately developed, functioning with little conscious effort on our part and allowing us to experience the beauty that surrounds and engulfs us. They are there and we pay little attention to them because they just do their assigned task.

The Beauty of Pain

One aspect of our sensory system has a double edge—it is both a positive alert system and also a cause of great discomfort. Pain, while largely unpleasant and unsought, is beautiful in its own way. Sensitivity to pain is calibrated differently for different areas of the body and is determined by the area of use. The fingers are very sensitive to pain because they do many things that require a delicate touch, so to prevent injury, pressure must be reported quickly. The soles of our feet are calloused and very tough from walking on them and therefore more pressure is required before pain is felt.

Philip Yancey, in his book *Where Is God When It Hurts?*, relates his experiences with Dr. Paul Brand working with people with leprosy, a disease that destroys the ability to feel pain. Patients with leprosy get burns and other injuries to toes and feet, fingers and hands without any awareness of the injury occurring. In fact, they can put a digit or limb in a fire, watch it burn and never feel it. Yancey quotes Dr. Brand on pain: "Thank God for inventing pain! I don't think he could have done a better job. It's beautiful."[4] Yancey goes on to say, "Pain is not God's great goof. The sensation of pain is a gift—the gift nobody wants. More than anything, pain should be viewed as a communication network . . . a remarkable network of pain sensors . . . with the singular purpose of keeping us from injury."[5]

Human Creativity and Beauty

The beauty of God is extended through the best of His created works—people—as we design, fashion, and create our own works of beauty and ingenuity. In fact, our desire to create is itself part of God's image in us: just as His very being bubbled over in the creation of the world, so we "bubble over" as we imagine and create. Every time we create, we reflect God's image in us, and we represent something of God's truth in what we make; these truths include goodness, order, harmony, and beauty.

Except in rare circumstances, like Noah's ark and Israel's tabernacle, humanity has been on its own to assess its needs, design the necessary items, and then make them using people's creative abilities. Craftsmen design shelters, clothing, tools, and furnishings. They consider color, style, and materials, using the earth's raw materials to fashion the ideas in their minds. Over the centuries people have become very skilled and creative in developing more efficient ways of making things and of making them more attractive. In countries like ours, we have more disposable income with which to decorate the interiors of our homes according to our tastes. We select floor and wall coverings, window treatments, furniture styles, and color schemes. Each home speaks to the creative abilities and beauty tastes of the owners—or the professionals hired to help.

Our creative ability and our appreciation for beauty change over the span of our lives. As children we invent playmates, shape clay, and draw stick figure families—masterpieces! By the time we reach high school, many of us are skilled musicians, rehearsed actors, or insightful writers. Others are mastering cooking skills while yet others have cultivated carpentry skills. Our creativity allows us to change, make new, remodel, and even acquire new skills for as long as we are able. This is a wonderful ability that God has granted us.

There are thousands of people groups—each with its own language or dialect, cultural values, artifacts, customs, and level of development that reflect its unique creative tastes and abilities. No one people group has a monopoly on creativity or works of beauty. This almost endless array of

---

4. Yancey, *Where Is God When It Hurts?*, 31.
5. Ibid., 34.

human creative ability mirrors the vastness of what God has provided in the natural world.

The Culmination of Human Beauty—the Arts

> Finally, brothers,
> whatever is true, whatever is noble,
> whatever is right, whatever is pure,
> whatever is lovely, whatever is admirable—
> if anything is excellent or praiseworthy—
> think about such things. (Phil 4:8)

The arts take us into a special arena of creativity and beauty. Art is an arena where excellence is prized, personal acclaim is often the goal, and top artists become "stars." Nicholas Wolterstorff identifies the eight major arts as music, poetry, drama, literary fiction, visual depiction, ballet and modern dance, film, and sculpture.[6] As we consider these, examples come to mind that illustrate their beauty as works of art: Beethoven's Fifth Piano Concerto; *The Nutcracker Suite* by Tchaikovsky; Dante's *Divine Comedy* from the 1300s; Shakespeare's plays of the 1500 and 1600s; John Bunyan's allegorical *The Pilgrim's Progress*; da Vinci's *Mona Lisa*; the ceiling of the Sistine Chapel by Michelangelo. Each of these works has been enjoyed and appreciated by people for hundreds of years. They are recognized, along with many other works, as being of superior quality; their endurance owes itself to their quality.

What is the value of the arts to a culture, and especially to a culture such as ours, preoccupied with pragmatic considerations? There are several answers to this question. First, the arts allow us to rejoice in excellence—excellence developed out of God-endowed aptitudes in a particular area. Artists are gifted people, masters in their areas of artistic ability. Their works evoke awe and respect and accolades from adoring publics. Listening to, viewing, or reading their works gives great pleasure because the artists have created their works for just that purpose: "to be delightful in themselves."[7]

Second, the arts provide vehicles of enjoyment for us during our leisure time. Participation might involve listening, viewing, or actively pursuing some combination of the following:

- Music: We enjoy music at concerts and in the privacy of our own homes. We can also enjoy music by joining music groups at all levels of society and using our musical abilities for the enjoyment of others.

---

6. Wolterstorff, *Art in Action*, 6.
7. Ryken, *Culture in Christian Perspective*, 37.

- Drama: We can pay to attend theater performances, the best place to experience drama, or we can surf channels from the comfort of our own couches. Those of us with dramatic ability can participate in local drama groups and perform for local audiences.
- Art: A visit to an art gallery allows for an unhurried viewing of the work of artists. To fully appreciate art, we have to take time to reflect on the piece, noting what the artist is portraying, what human experience is expressed, and how it is being expressed. Then we can quietly applaud the artistry and thank God for gifting artists to produce such expressive works for our enjoyment and contemplation.
- Literature: The beautifully crafted stories of great writers draw us into their world of imagery. We become involved in the life of the main character, her experiences, emotions, and thoughts, until the story is resolved. These stories resonate with our own humanity, and in a profound way enrich our lives.

What is the value of the arts to a culture? The arts represent the soul and true wealth of a culture. Contrary to what economists might say, the wealth of a culture isn't measured by the stock market; it is measured by the cultivation and expression of its corporate imagination. Its values are often expressed through the arts.

People gifted in the arts have been endowed with their artistic aptitudes by God, just as He has endowed people in other areas. For some the use of their ability becomes a life work, while for most it is a hobby or service expressed through participation in a community organization. Regardless, artistic skills are gifts of God, as is all of life. Because they are from God, artistic gifts should be shared so others can celebrate God's gifts of beauty. Even the work of artists who do not acknowledge God should be applauded and appreciated as gifts of God's common grace, lavished on the just and the unjust.

The Fall

Humans were created to image God in both our appreciation for and our generation of beauty. The breadth and depth of our creative potential enlarges every time another person is born—we each offer our uniqueness to the human enterprise. But like everything else about us and our world, our capacity for beauty was marred and broken by the fall. Because the ideas and the motivations for every creative work originate in the heart, the very depth of the human being, "the arts, which speak so subjectively and so very personally regarding who and what we are in relation to our Maker are very vulnerable to the distortion that sin has brought into the world."[8]

This distortion is evident in at least three ways: (1) the kind of beauty that is most important to us—external beauty; (2) an imbalance between form and function; and (3) the perversion of that which is beautiful.

A Focus on External Beauty

The beauty of people, according to human definition, is determined by physical proportions, hairstyle, and facial features. While no one can totally avoid making judgments by these standards, the fall corrupted our ability to look beyond them. Now, we primarily judge the beauty of people by their external appearance.

Sin obstructs our view of true human beauty—illustrated by God through the lives of several biblical characters, including Ruth, a non-Israelite who married an Israelite living in her homeland of Moab because of famine in his hometown, Bethlehem. In the course of time, all the men of the Israelite family died, leaving the mother, Naomi, a desolate widow. Naomi decided to return to Bethlehem, but urged her daughters-in-law to stay and remarry in Moab. Despite Naomi's urging, Ruth left her homeland and went to Bethlehem with Naomi, where she vowed to identify with Naomi's people, to serve her God, and only be separated from Naomi by death. Ruth—about whose physical appearance the Bible is silent—gleaned grain in the field of Boaz, a relative, and found herself favored by him because he recognized her inner beauty (Ruth 2:11–12). Because of Ruth's noble character (Ruth 3:11), Boaz was eager and willing to fulfill his responsibility as kinsman-redeemer to her and Naomi.

Because of the fall, we don't usually see people the way Boaz saw Ruth. Instead, our perspective on beauty is misaligned at best and perverted at worst. We spend too much money on the latest styles, worry excessively about the shape and size of our aging bodies, and spend more time getting ready in the morning than talking with God.

An Imbalance between Form and Function

Another way we display our fallen sense of beauty is in our imbalance between form and function. Most often, we disregard form in favor of function. Americans especially, it seems, have perfected the "art" of function over form: the ultimate standard we use is whether something works. Appearance, while we may think it is somewhat important, falls far behind

---

8. Gaebelein, *The Christian, the Arts, and Truth*, 75.

our demand for function. Of course, it is important that the things we design and make *work*—who needs a car that doesn't run or house with a faulty foundation?—but we often stop at function. Consider the Pinto, early solar panel heating, and the shallow plotlines of reality TV. Consider in Christianity the contrast between medieval cathedrals or the Sistine Chapel and modern "multipurpose space" in churches; or consider the contrast between literary classics and mediocre Christian fiction. When we produce merely out of "bottom line" motivation, we are imbalanced, and we disregard the importance of beauty. In the classroom, this tendency appears in hastily scribbled pictures and poorly written essays produced just to make the grade, and it shows itself in a half-hearted analysis of literature and lifeless recitation of a poetry assignment. The old motto we all heard repeatedly from Mom—"A job worth doing is worth doing well"—applies here.

Other times, however, we swing out of balance in the other direction, focusing on "beauty" or form over function. We design, create, and pursue things that may attain a certain acceptable appearance but are absolutely useless—or even harmful. Consider the corset, high-heeled shoes, and the craze for tanned skin. This notion dovetails with the first effect of the fall that we discussed—the concern for external beauty above inner beauty. While less prominent, we see this imbalance in the classroom as well when students turn in "beautiful" assignments that entirely miss the mark of the requirements—well-written essays that don't answer the question or carefully rehearsed skits with lots of props but little connection to the topic at hand.

The Perversion of What Is Beautiful

A third manifestation of our fallen sense of beauty is the perversion of that which is beautiful, most evident in our culture in pornographic materials (again, dovetailing with our priority of external beauty), the glorification of violence in movies, and the lewd, crass humor that dominates prime-time television.

Artists—whether visual or verbal—who display human experiences primarily in terms of violence, vulgar language, and sexual relationships may communicate reality, but they also feed our fallen appetites for such perversion of beauty. The Bible itself includes violence, vulgar language, and sexual language, but not simply for their own sake as most often happens in modern media. God sets the standard for the inclusion of such details by showing "reticence in portraying sex as part of a thorough analysis of human experience," rather than "linger[ing] over details of the human body or sexual activity."[9] When the Bible includes violence, vulgarity, and sexual language, it reminds us of humanity's fallenness and the devastating effects of sin on God's world.

Redemption

God's beauty is perfect while human-generated beauty is flawed; sinful people create and decide what is beautiful based on their hearts and worldviews. Because we are sinful creatures, we focus on external beauty, cannot balance form and function, and pervert that which is beautiful. Sin taints every work of art—literature, music, sculpture, painting, dance, and drama.

While every human, redeemed or not, has the capacity to create beauty, Christians ought to be the ones generating the greatest human beauty; of all people, those redeemed and rescued from the world system can appreciate the beauty of the Creator and reflect Him in their own creativity.

Redemption paves the way for us to appreciate God's beauty and His value of beauty, recognize where genuine beauty is found, and commit to cultivating beauty in everything we do.

Recognizing and Revealing God's Beauty

Artists are keen observers of reality and of human experiences, capturing and presenting a concrete expression of reality in images and symbols rather than in abstract or propositional statements. Redeemed artists ought to produce works that display beauty, redemption, the good, order, balance, harmony, and symmetry—all reflections of God and His works. Such art reveals something about God, just as the natural world does: it shows us that God is a God of order, balance, harmony, recognizable forms, beauty, and symmetry.

Works of art often incarnate an idea, an instance of an event into something concrete and sensory. God did this when He incarnated Himself in human form to show and tell us what He is really like and what matters to Him. In a very limited way, we are to be "through-a-glass-darkly" incarnations of what God is like and in doing so we show to those who observe us that God is loving, patient, kind, and merciful.

In the Old Testament God gave His people some "art projects" that, in addition to providing a place to worship, also showcased God's glory

---

9. Ryken, *Culture*, 243–44.

and beauty. The tabernacle that was constructed in the wilderness was adorned with colorful fabrics, utensils of hammered gold and furniture of bronze, and the exquisite ark of the covenant, the symbol of God's presence made of acacia wood overlaid with gold. (The directions for building the tabernacle fill nearly fifty chapters in the Old Testament, while the creation of the entire world fills only two!) Its construction and the care it required were intended to remind the redeemed people of God's holiness, beauty, and character. It also reminded the people of their special relationship to Him as His redeemed people. While we are not working with divine blueprints today, nonetheless everything we create has the capacity to reflect the Creator—both to us and to others.

A Focus on Inner Beauty

Redeemed people, while not immune to the lures of physical beauty, are called to look beyond, to see deeper, to value above all the cultivation of inner beauty. Just in case we miss it in the narrative accounts of Scripture, God spells out what makes someone beautiful in 1 Peter 3:3–4 where He says to women, specifically wives, "Your beauty should not come from outward adornment, such as braided hair and the wearing of gold jewelry and fine clothes. Instead, it should be that of your inner self, the unfading beauty of a gentle and quiet spirit, which is of great worth in God's sight." God is not opposed to gold jewelry and fine clothes, but they are not ultimately what produce beauty.

God also addresses husbands in this context: "Husbands, in the same way be considerate as you live with your wives, and treat them with respect as the weaker partner and as heirs with you of the gracious gift of life, so that nothing will hinder your prayers" (1 Pet 3:7). Christian husbands were duty bound to hold a high regard for their wives by protecting, respecting, and loving them because they shared the common gift of eternal life. A husband and wife joining together in united prayer is a part of the beauty of the marriage relationship.

The context of this instruction is the larger issue of submission: all believers to authorities, slaves to their masters, wives to their husbands, and husbands to their wives. Some of the best manifestations of the beautiful life—and those most scorned by fallen humanity—are moral purity and loving respect. Clothes, hairstyles, and accessories are attractive and acceptable, but they cannot ultimately compete with character. Beauty emanates from inside, who we are at the very core of our beings.

A Commitment to Cultivating Beauty

Finally, those redeemed and rescued from the world's fallen values have every reason to commit themselves to the cultivation of beauty in whatever way they can—in their relationships, in their homes, in their yards, in their jobs, in their churches, in their hobbies. The tasks we do, the ways we spend our time are not, ultimately, for ourselves. Rather, everything we do is part of worshiping a holy, beautiful God, a God who calls us to reflect more and more clearly what He is like. We cannot reflect such a God through shoddy workmanship, surface friendships, hastily finished projects, overgrown yards, and messy homes. Everything we touch is a potential means to image the creativity and beauty of our God.

The cultivation of beauty—leaving the places we go and the people we know better for having been in contact with us—is a high and holy calling. It is not one we often ponder as Christians, but it is one of the most expansive ways we image our God.

Beauty and School Subjects

Life in Christ demands constant vigilance and vigorous personal censorship. The admonition of Paul in Philippians 4:8 to think on things that are true, honest, just, pure, lovely, and of good report provides guidelines for guarding our hearts and minds. It also provides a helpful, concise framework for teachers shaping their students' understanding of beauty. Beauty crosses the curriculum in that students produce works of their own minds for every subject; every assignment is an open door for creativity and careful work. We, however, are going to focus on those that specifically fall under the arts—literature, drama, music, and visual depiction.

Literature and Drama—the Art of Words

As students pass through the grades, they develop their levels of language proficiency and their love (or hatred) of language. For most students, language usage becomes utilitarian. But for a few, language becomes a passion; they have to write. They have to express themselves through prose, poetry, and drama. They become artists and their medium is literature, words that create an art form. Our task here is obvious: focus on the essential skills of good writing, direct them to models of good writing, and teach them how to find good examples of writing for the rest of their lives.

While not every student will develop this love—nor have this ability—it is important that our students learn to recognize and appreciate good literature. For the rest of their lives, they will encounter "literature," good stories told through books, drama, or cinematography. Literature reflects the culture. Much of contemporary storytelling glorifies and approves of immorality, realistic violence, and crude and blasphemous language, yet Christians participate in these stories almost as much as their unbelieving neighbors. Students with a truly biblical worldview should be taught to discern what is good literature and what is bad literature, based on how each reflects the God of beauty. We cannot make their viewing and reading decisions for them, but we must equip them to recognize the "non-beautiful" while understanding what it means to love and image a holy, beautiful God.

Music—the Art of Sounds

Music, the beauty of sound, has a universal appeal and has been part of culture since the beginning. In Genesis 4:21 we read of Jubal, "the father of all who play the harp and the flute." Throughout the Old Testament, the people of Israel composed songs to celebrate important events in their life as the people of God (Psalms). The exodus (Exod 15), Israel's victory over Jabin (Judg 4–5), the return of the ark to Jerusalem (1 Chron 15), the completion of the temple (1 Chron 25), and all the events that prompted David to pen his psalms to God. The New Testament continues the theme of music among the people of God in their churches (Eph 5:19; Col 3:16) and around the throne of God (Rev 4:6–14). Music is part of culture, and especially Christian culture.

Music is taught as a school subject for everyone, for personal enjoyment and often for public presentation. Recorders, school bands and orchestras, choir concerts, and special singing groups are all part of a student's musical experience. This involvement in musical activities brings to the fore those with special ability to sing or play for the enjoyment of others and to the glory of God.

Music, created by God, can be used for good or evil. Again, the task of Christian teachers is to steer our students into an understanding of God's creation and the appropriate human response to Him. Just as with literature, we cannot make our students' decisions, but we must equip them to recognize the "non-beautiful" while understanding what it means to love and image a holy, beautiful God.

Visual Depiction—the Art of Shapes

Children begin in early childhood to express themselves with simple materials and designs. They scribble with large crayons, make lines with a fat pencil, squeeze Play-Doh, and stack blocks. Children depict things that are of importance to them—a birthday party, a day at the beach, Mommy and Daddy. They are always thinking, observing, evaluating, imagining, and talking about their thoughts, sometimes even as they depict them.

When children begin school they have expanded and more guided opportunities for visual depiction. They become acquainted with new materials like finger paints and easels. As they progress through the grades they learn the elements of good art composition, and those with artistic aptitude rise to the top. Student projects begin to show promise for future work in some aspect of the wider field of art, graphic arts, architecture, sculpture, pottery making, and even painting on canvas. No matter their aptitude, however, all students will develop some sort of interest in visual depiction for enjoyment as a leisure time activity or a hobby, but as with literature and music, they need to filter their choices through the grid of Philippians 4:8—that which is true, honest, just, pure, lovely, and of good report.

Conclusion

Beauty surrounds us: it is everywhere in nature and in people, gifts of God the beautiful Creator. To be sure, the fallen world has tainted, spoiled, and perverted God's lavish gifts of beauty. As redeemed images of Him, we strive to appreciate and display the finest of God's beauty in our own lives and in what we produce and enjoy. As teachers we work to help our students better understand the beauty of God Himself and His creation, and in light of that, to leave their stamp of beauty on everything they touch and everyone they meet.

Summary of Truths

God's Beauty

1. We see God's beauty in everything He made: the world and all that is in it, including us.
2. Everything He made was good and perfect, because He is good and perfect. His creation reflects Him.
3. God made a beautiful place of detail and variety for us to enjoy.

4. God declared the earth to be good and *very* good; it was adequate for its intended purpose.
    a. He made plants in every shape, size, and color—a feast for the senses. They are each perfectly designed to fulfill specific functions.
    b. The world is full of thousands of living creatures, each intricately designed for its environment as well as for our use and enjoyment.
    c. The landscapes and seascapes designed by God are each His handiwork, intended to inspire our awe, provide for our needs, and be a pleasure to us.
    d. The heavens with its stars, clouds, moon, and sun declare to all regions and peoples of the world God's incomparable glory.
5. We can see the beauty of God in who He is. The beauty of God is a theme that flows through the Scriptures from Genesis to Revelation. We best understand this beauty in the way God relates to us.
    a. God is beautiful in His holiness, and because He is holy, we are given the chance to be holy too.
    b. God is beautiful in His love and mercy, and we see this most clearly in the gift of redemption He offers to us, sinners, through Jesus Christ.
    c. God is beautiful in His longsuffering, patiently forgiving us and helping us live in ways that please Him.
    d. God is beautiful in His joy, and this joy is multiplied by us—God takes pleasure in us.
6. God's beauty, evident in His creation and in His relationship to us, should prompt our worship and awe, and it should encourage us to reflect beauty to those around us.
7. We can see God's beauty in the way He has made us.
    a. He created us in His image, and therefore we are capable of producing beauty ourselves and of enjoying the beauty others create.
    b. God designed our five senses, allowing us to soak in and delight in the creativity around us.
    c. God equipped our bodies to alert us to pain, a way to protect what He has made.
    d. We have the God-given ability to assess human needs, design the necessary items, and then make them.

    e. The things we each create reflect our individuality, another God-given characteristic that results in an endless array of creative possibility.
8. The arts manifest the best of human creative ability—humanity saying, "It is good" of the things we have made. Even those who do not acknowledge God in their creative abilities reflect Him, probably against their wishes!
9. The arts also provide means for us to enjoy participation in areas of beauty: we can sing, act, sculpt, paint, read, write—all for the pure delight of it.

Beauty Has Been Corrupted by the Fall

1. While humans were designed to reflect God in His beauty, sin distorts our ability to create and enjoy beauty.
2. Because of sin, we judge beauty by external appearance, no longer recognizing that inner character is the truest reflection of beauty.
3. Because of sin, we do not know how to appropriately balance form and function—an ability so evident in God's creation of the world. We tend to emphasize one over the other, and this can result in making things that are useless, shoddy, or even harmful.
4. Because we are sinful, we pervert what is beautiful. This is evident in pornography, sexually explicit television, glorified violence, and cheap literature.

Beauty Can Be Redeemed

1. Jesus' redemptive work on the cross paves the way for the redemption of beauty in our lives as well.
2. Christians should be producing the best of everything in the arts because God is restoring our view of His beauty and our beauty.
3. Christians are best equipped to recognize genuine beauty, that which flows from a transformed heart and mind.
4. The beauty of our inner character is most important, and the Bible shows us how to be more and more beautiful from the inside out.
5. Christians have the most reason of anybody to produce beauty in everything they touch—their homes, their occupations, their hobbies, their relationships: we reflect God's beauty in the beauty that we create.

Beauty in the Classroom

1. Introducing students to the arts is a vital—and incredibly Christian—aspect of the curriculum; learning how to recognize and create beauty lies at the heart of who we are as God's image-bearers.
2. Evaluating beautiful literature (and its offspring—movies) requires identifying its worldview and values and then assessing it against God's standards for beauty.
3. Learning how to appreciate beautiful music and to master musical instruments should lie at the foundation of arts education.
4. We begin creating visual art as soon as we pick up crayons; students need to learn to identify beauty and non-beauty in art.
5. Philippians 4:8 forms a grid through which the arts can be filtered: are they true? honest? just? pure? lovely? of good report?

Teaching Tips

1. Beauty in the Bible. Identify characters in the Bible whose physical appearance is described. What does the Bible say about them and how does their appearance factor into the story, if at all. (Characters include Rebekah, Rachel, Baby Moses, Samson, Saul, Bathsheba, Esther, Abigail, David, the "Servant" of Isaiah 53, and Absalom.) Identify characters whose external appearance is not described but who are characterized by "inner beauty," male or female. (Upper elementary)

2. A Bouquet of Flowers. Have students bring in pictures of flowers, or, depending on the season of the year, have them bring in pressed/dried flowers from home. Collect additional pictures on your own to supplement what they have so you have a sizeable collection. As a large group, or in small groups, have students arrange the flowers according to colors or shapes or size, etc. Note the variety and the beauty in the flowers. This activity could follow a lesson on the parts of flowers and their functions; highlight the variety of ways God has made flowers to perform similar functions. (Lower to middle elementary)

3. The Eye of the Beholder. Using television ads, examples of local architecture (good and bad), elements of your city's layout, and other aspects of American culture, discuss with your students what values Americans exhibit when it comes to appearance, convenience, cost, comfort, etc. Where do we see "form" over "function"? Where do we see "function" over "form"? What are biblical values in these areas, and

where do we see such values reflected in our culture or in our lives? How can we cultivate these values? (Junior high and high school)

4. Beauty on the Big Screen. (This activity will work best over a period of time, perhaps as a supplement to another area of study.) Select a film that artfully tells a story (e.g., *Amazing Grace*, *It's a Wonderful Life*, or *Spider-Man 2*) or a film of a classic book (e.g., *Les Miserables*, *Jane Eyre*, or *Ben Hur*) and watch it in class. (Try to find something everybody hasn't already seen.) Discuss the aspects of it that are artful, reasons it has or is likely to stand the test of time for its quality. How does it reflect beauty? Then select a film that has little lasting value (but is still "appropriate" for partial viewing in class) although it may have been madly popular in its time (e.g., *Transformers*, *Evan Almighty*, or any number of movies at your local video store!). Watch it in class and discuss how the two movies differ. How does the second example fall short of "beauty"? You could do the same activity with television dramas, sitcoms, and reality TV. (Junior high and high school)

5. Standing on Their Shoulders. Each generation adds to the learning of previous generations (we "stand on their shoulders"), and it is important for our students to appreciate the history that leads to present-day disciplines. Compile a list of Christians who have worked in your subject area, and as part of your semester's assigned workload, have students read a biography of a Christian in your field and report in writing or to the class what the person accomplished, how faith influenced his or her studies, and what legacy he or she has left. (Junior high and high school)

Additional Resources[10]

1. Myers, Kenneth A. *All God's Children and Blue Suede Shoes: Christians and Popular Culture.* Wheaton: Crossway Books, 1989. Myers examines the roots, assumptions, and practices of pop culture, a shallow replacement for fine arts and "high culture." He provides a discerning perspective on how Christians can reflect Christ in a culture of diversion.

2. Niebuhr, H. Richard. *Christ and Culture.* New York: Harper, 1951. While not directly related to "beauty," this book indirectly affects every aspect of the arts by asking how Christ is relevant in and to culture today. The answer determines the way in which Christians engage in culture.

10. Thanks to Bethany Wood for her help compiling this list.

3. Ryken, Leland. *Culture in Christian Perspective: A Door to Understanding and Enjoying the Arts.* Portland, OR: Multnomah Press, 1986. Ryken has numerous titles that contribute to the discussion about creativity and culture. In this book, he encourages Christians to fully enjoy the wealth of the arts as creators and participants, rather than withdrawing from the arts because of their misuse.

4. Sayers, Dorothy L. *The Mind of the Maker.* San Francisco: Harper San Franciso, 1941. A brilliant work, this book reflects on the process of creating and the depths of theological truth inherent in this process.

5. Schaeffer, Francis. *Art and the Bible: Two Essays.* 2d ed. Downers Grove, IL: InterVarsity Press, 2007. This brief but powerful book is a foundational work in the study of Christianity and the arts. In his classic work, Schaeffer explains why "the Christian is the one whose imagination should fly beyond the stars."

6. Schaeffer, Franky. *Addicted to Mediocrity: 20th Century Christians and the Arts.* Revised ed. Wheaton: Crossway Books, 1985. Although creativity is an essential aspect of the Christian life in that it images God, Christians in current culture have not done a stellar job at reflecting God. Schaeffer's critique offers a way forward to excellence in artistic expression.

7. Wolters, Albert M. *Creation Regained: Biblical Basics for a Reformational Worldview.* 2d ed. Grand Rapids: Eerdmans, 2005. Wolters's discussion of the creation-fall-redemption grid that governs a Christian worldview is a helpful tool for analyzing everything in culture. By determining the original design for God's created order, a critic can also determine what is fallen about its current state.

8. Wolterstorff, Nicholas. *Art in Action.* Grand Rapids: Eerdmans, 1980. A lucid and original writer, Wolterstorff takes on the significance of art in daily life in this book. Rooted in Christian theology, he discusses aesthetics, a philosophy of art, and the role of art in life.

5
Ultimate Issues

Each fall Wendy's fifth graders learned Psalm 139, adding two verses a week until they could say the entire psalm. All went well until they reached verses 11–12: "If I say, 'Surely the darkness will hide me and the light become night around me,' even the darkness will not be dark to You, the night will shine like the day, for darkness is as light to you." It reads all right to adults on paper, but when you're ten it's a brain bender to remember and recite. Every Friday morning for eight weeks, she'd listen to mutilated variations on the themes of light and darkness, and more often than not, she'd say the words with them until they had stumbled through to clear sailing in verse 13.

Weekly Bible memory is just one way Christian school teachers teach the Bible. We work hard to help our students be biblically literate: knowledgeable of the Bible's narrative, major characters, primary themes, and even the order of the books. We also hope for some level of literacy in church history: awareness of names like Martin Luther and Jonathan Edwards, and familiarity with terms like the Council of Trent and the Reformation. To this end, we have our students memorize verses, make timelines, don costumes for skits, and do biographical book reports.

But we all know that the facts aren't enough. We want our students to adopt the values and apply the truths of Scripture. We pray that "Sword Drills" lead to a love for the breadth of Scripture. We hope that recitation of the Ten Commandments translates into devoted love for God and compassionate concern for others. We long for our students to marry well, parent well, and become exemplary employees.

We want them to find the Solid Rock in times of need. When airplanes fly into buildings or when hurricanes drown cities, we want them to cling to something beyond this life. When their lives are shattered by disease, death, or divorce, we pray they can see more than what lies in front of them. By our responses to adversity, we teach our students how to grieve, but not as those without hope. While we grieve, we also pray our students will find the solid ground when the very foundations shift.

Really, what we desire more than anything is for our students to meet and love Jesus. Wendy was reminded of this one day when David slipped up to her desk. "Miss Widder," he quietly said, "I just finished this." She looked at the picture David, a wisp of a child, held out to her and was stunned by the emotion on the page. In his soft pencil style, David had sketched the crucifixion, and with brimming eyes he explained the significance of each detail he had included. His picture was more than the facts Wendy had taught about the cross; it was David's internalization of the Truth.

While biblical truth is hopefully integrated into everything we teach from kindergarten through twelfth grade, in Bible class we explicitly teach the Book. When our students arrive in high school, we begin formally teaching them about other beliefs in the world community. We acquaint them with a variety of religions and philosophies, all the while wrestling against the forces of religious pluralism and tolerance. We struggle to help them love people with beliefs and values so different from their own, how to "hate sin but love sinners." We encounter the culture wars at every turn and are reminded how many powers are pulling for the hearts and minds of our students. In these encounters, we wonder: Have we given them enough? Have we planted and watered the right seeds? Which direction will they turn when they leave our classrooms? Do they really know God? And thus comes perhaps the biggest test of a teacher's faith: entrusting to God the precious lives that sit before us each day, trusting Him to make the seeds grow.

Introduction

DEATH AND taxes—the two things said to be certain. Unless our students are headed into tax-related careers, they are not much interested in taxes. But death is a topic of interest as soon as a child is old enough to understand that people die. Where do they go? Where will *I* go? There are few, if any, questions bigger than this one.

As Christian teachers, we care a great deal about how our students answer this question. We care because we are concerned about what will happen to the precious ones we teach, but we also care because we know that how they answer this question determines to a great extent how they will live. The answer to the question of death creates a framework in which students answer the other "big questions" of life: What is true? How do I know what to believe? What makes something right or wrong? Who decides? Does my life really matter? Is there a purpose to life? A full menu of options is available to our students as they attempt to answer these questions for themselves, but only the Christian worldview will provide them with a coherent framework for living with purpose and for dying. Our job is to make that framework as clear to them as possible—and pray with Elijah's fervency that God draws them to Himself.

We live in a world that includes God in many of its worldviews. People are compelled to pray when they find themselves hard-pressed for help, and the better ones among the earth's inhabitants try to obey some version of the Golden Rule. To most of these people, it doesn't matter who you think "God" is: Allah or some great spiritual force or the Old Testament God—"God," by any other name, is still "God." But, the Christian worldview says it does matter, monumentally. It matters because of the God-man, Jesus.

Wendy attended a Steve Green concert some time after September 11, and as Steve introduced his final song, "A Mighty Fortress," he related a story. Invited to sing Martin Luther's great hymn at a national service in the days following the tragedy, he declined when he was told he could not sing the second verse:

> Did we in our own strength confide, our striving
>   would be losing.
> Were not the right Man on our side, the man of
>   God's own choosing:
> Dost ask who that may be? Christ Jesus, it is He;
> Lord Sabaoth, His Name, from age to age the same,
> And He must win the battle.

Every verse in the hymn refers to God, but except to extreme secularists or atheists, "God" is not controversial. And even the most diehard of these opponents will often join hands in "prayer" during tragedies. Verse two, however, brings Jesus into the picture, defining God a little too narrowly for most people's comfort. Many of the world's believers in "God" would just as soon leave Jesus out of things—or say He was a great moral teacher and leave it at that. We can all get along better that way.

That may be true, insofar as it goes, but leaving Jesus out is like squeezing our eyes tightly shut, sticking our fingers in our ears, and singing a tune to drown out reality. Jesus cannot be ignored—at least, not indefinitely. Josh McDowell paraphrases the great C. S. Lewis by laying out the issue: Jesus was either a liar or a lunatic, or He was (and is) Lord. Lewis famously says,

> I am trying here to prevent anyone saying the really foolish thing that people often say about Him: "I'm ready to accept Jesus as a great moral teacher, but I don't accept His claim to be God." That is the one thing we must not say. A man who was merely a man and said the sort of things Jesus said would not be a great moral teacher. He would either be a lunatic—on a level with the man

who says he is a poached egg—or else he would be the Devil of Hell. . . . You can shut Him up for a fool, you can spit at him and kill Him as a demon; or you can fall at His feet and call Him Lord and God. But let us not come up with any patronising nonsense about His being a great human teacher. He has not left that open to us. He did not intend to.[1]

Jesus lived—plenty of historical evidence attests to this. He died and He arose from the dead; again, plenty of historical evidence attests to this. Sidestepping Him, as most of the world does, will not remove the reality of His person or activity from the annals of history; nor will it prevent His future impact on the world. How we deal with Jesus determines how we live, and eventually, how we will die. In this chapter, we will ask, "Who is Jesus, in the Old Testament and the New, and how does the answer affect my life?"

Who Was Jesus?

So, who was Jesus? Who *is* Jesus? What is it about Him that drove His followers like men possessed after His death and during the two thousand years since? In the Gospels we learn about Jesus' earthly life, but from the rest of the New and the Old Testament we learn much more about His activity from eternity past and into eternity future. He is all over the Book: in types and prophecies, as an active character, and as the central theme of the entire Story. When He finally appears in the flesh, He does so as the climax of the Old Testament plotline.

New Testament—"You Are to Give Him the Name Jesus"

Matthew and Luke record the miraculous events of Jesus' birth from the womb of the young virgin, Mary. His childhood and adolescence are all but skipped over in the Gospels, and Jesus enters the scene again at the age of thirty when He began His ministry among His people, the Jews, in the land of Palestine. He performed countless miracles, tangled with the religious leaders, and trained twelve men to be His disciples. The culmination of His earthly ministry included His death by Roman crucifixion—a cruel death reserved for the worst criminals—and His resurrection three days later. During the next forty days, Jesus appeared in a glorified body to many of His followers and disciples, whom He instructed to carry His message of salvation to the ends of the earth. Then He was gone, ascending to

---

1. C. S. Lewis, *Mere Christianity*, 40–41.

heaven before their eyes, and His disciples got busy proclaiming the incredible news: Jesus' death and resurrection made new life available! Before long, the good news—the gospel—had spread throughout Palestine and neighboring countries. These tumultuous but exciting days are recorded in the book of Acts.

Wherever the gospel was preached, its acceptance produced groups of believers, little churches. Their Bible was the Old Testament, and they certainly knew the oral accounts of Jesus' life, teachings, deeds, and gospel message. As these believers struggled to translate their faith into everyday living, Paul, Peter, James, Jude, and John wrote letters (our New Testament Epistles) to help them.

The last appearance of Jesus in the New Testament is in its final pages, the Revelation of Jesus Christ, the book written by an exiled John on the island of Patmos. In John's wild apocalyptic ride through the future, Jesus is the Lamb slain and He is the Judge of all the earth. At the end of time, He will return to the earth and set up His kingdom where He will live with His people forever:

> Then I saw a new heaven and a new earth, for the first heaven and the first earth had passed away, and there was no longer any sea. I saw the Holy City, the new Jerusalem, coming down out of heaven from God, prepared as a bride beautifully dressed for her husband. And I heard a loud voice from the throne saying, "Now the dwelling of God is with men, and He will live with them. They will be his people, and God Himself will be with them and be their God. He will wipe every tear from their eyes. There will be no more death or mourning or crying or pain, for the old order of things has passed away."
>
> He who was seated on the throne said, "I am making everything new!" Then he said, "Write this down, for these words are trustworthy and true." (Rev 21:1–5)

Old Testament—"Beginning with Moses and All the Prophets . . ."

Shortly after His resurrection, Jesus talked with some disciples who didn't recognize Him. They were confused about the recent events, and Jesus explained things they should have known about Him and His mission— "beginning with Moses and all the prophets, he explained to them what was said in all the Scriptures concerning himself" (Luke 24:27; many a pastor and teacher has since lamented that Jesus' words were not recorded by Luke.) God the Son is present from the first pages of Genesis and through the final pages of Malachi. He is there, but His presence is somewhat veiled until the New Testament pulls back the curtain. Thus, our "search" for Jesus in the Old Testament will follow the same course as the Bible itself: we begin with the narrative of the Old Testament and then, when we arrive in the New Testament, we will look back to see Him.

The Story of Jesus, from Beginning to End

Setting the Stage

The Story, familiar by now, opens with the splendor of creation but quickly dissolves into the despair wrought by sin. God created a perfect universe, but before its managers had a chance to get very far into their responsibilities, they fell prey to Satan's temptation. The necessary judgment was quickly pronounced on all three—Adam, Eve, and the serpent—but with a promise of hope for the human offenders: "And I will put enmity between you [the serpent] and the woman, and between your offspring and hers; he will crush your head, and you will strike his heel" (Gen 3:15). The promise that Satan would be defeated by the offspring of the woman casts a hopeful tenor over the pall of Old Testament failure. God did not forsake the people He had made in His likeness, and already by Genesis 3:15, He has initiated His program of redemption.

When we get to Exodus and Leviticus, God establishes the terms of His covenant with His special people, the descendants of Abraham, Isaac, and Jacob—the people of Israel. Focused on God's incomparable holiness, the covenant includes the Ten Commandments, some explication of how the Ten Commandments work, and an elaborate system of offerings. Each offering was designed to impress upon the people their sinfulness and God's holiness. The gulf between the two was immense and impossible for any person to close on their own.

God, however, had a great love for Israel, manifested in His choice of them to be "his treasured possession" (Deut 7:6–8). It was through this little nation that God would reveal Himself to the world and would ultimately send the Savior. Israel did nothing to merit or retain such favor; neither had they sought it. God, of His own will, chose them. Throughout their history, the Israelites repeatedly disobeyed God, rejected Him in favor of pagan gods, and were ever ungrateful for their special relationship. Yet God remained faithful.

Old Testament "Solutions"

Because of their continual sin, the people needed to pay regular penalties. God's penalty for sin was separation from Him, namely, death. People deserved death to pay the price of their sin, but God had a different plan. He provided substitutes to die in place of His people: unblemished animals sacrificed in a prescribed manner removed the guilt of the people's sin (Lev 1:4). Such offerings for sin were repeated many times by individuals throughout the year.

Then once a year, Israel observed a special Day of Atonement when the high priest made an offering for the collective sins of the people. He went into the Most Holy Place of the temple with the blood of a bull and sprinkled some of it on the atonement cover atop the ark of the covenant to atone for his own sin. Then he took the blood of a goat into the Most Holy Place and sprinkled it on the atonement cover for the sin of all the people. Finally, he took a second goat and, laying his hands on its head, he confessed the wickedness and rebellion of the Israelites. Then he sent the goat into the wilderness, a scapegoat that took the sins of the people far away (Lev 16:21–22) and restored the people to a right relationship with God.

The death of an animal and the sprinkling of its blood was the price sinners paid for reconciliation with God: something else took their punishment and turned away God's anger. While violent and bloody, this system had its own beauty—the fact that God Himself established and required its regular observance so that the people He loved could avert the wrath demanded by His holiness and justice. Through substitutionary deaths, the people's sins were removed and God's requirements for justice were satisfied.

But it was a limited system—both in terms of its extent of forgiveness and in terms of those who represented the people to God, the priests. The sacrifices were temporary solutions for sin: year after year, the people had to bring animals to atone for their sins. And those who offered the sacrifices for them were imperfect. The priests needed to atone for their own sins first. Then there were even priests who flagrantly abused their positions (see Nadab and Abihu [Lev 10], Eli's sons [1 Sam 2:12–36], and Hosea's harsh indictment of the priesthood [Hosea 4–5]). The Old Testament doesn't make a secret of the fact that the system and its administrators fell short of perfection.

But there are other systems and servants that fell short. Shortly after conquering the land God had promised to them, the Israelites entrapped themselves in a vicious cycle of sin (see the book of Judges). Finally the people cried out to the prophet Samuel to give them a king like all the surrounding nations had. Against his better judgment, but in line with God's plan, Samuel anointed Saul as the first king of Israel. Saul's tenure lasted for forty years, but long before his reign ended, his demise had begun. Replaced by God's choice, David, Saul finds little praise in the Old Testament. But even David, the standard by whom nearly all other kings are measured, fails to be faithful to both God and to His people. He commits adultery and murder, parents poorly, and watches his household tear itself apart on account of his sin. After the reign of David's son Solomon, the kingdom splits and only seven of a combined thirty-nine kings are said to follow God's ways, and some of these even receive a grudging commendation. The kings, representatives of the nation(s), fell short.

One more group of leaders emerges in the Old Testament: prophets. Beginning with Moses who spoke the words of God to the people, prophets played a major role in calling the people and their leaders to account. True prophets like Samuel, Isaiah, Amos, and others were not afraid to tell kings and peasants alike that they had failed to keep God's laws and that God would eventually bring judgment. At the risk of their own lives, these servants faithfully proclaimed words of God that applied to the immediate situation and those that wouldn't be fulfilled for years to come. Alongside these true prophets, however, false prophets tickled the people's ears, saying "Peace, peace," when there was no peace (Jer 6:14, 8:11) and "Is not the LORD among us? No disaster will come upon us" (Mic 3:11).

By the end of the Old Testament, all three groups of leaders have proven to be insufficient to meet the needs of the people. Sacrifices were still required, priests needed their own sacrifices, and some priests couldn't even be trusted. Kings were corrupt before the exile, and after the exile the kingship is nonexistent. Prophets couldn't always be trusted to speak God's word. The Old Testament ends with a gaping hole. Everything that has stood between the people and God has fallen short.

The Old Testament also concludes with dozens of loose ends. True prophets had spoken many things in the vein of Genesis 3:15, but many of these prophecies remained unrealized.

Putting the Pieces in Place

And so we turn the page to Matthew, and by the end of the first chapter, we have been introduced to someone unlike anybody we've met thus far in the Story—someone who was not "begotten" by any father and yet was born of a woman (Matt 1:16). In the person of Jesus, so named because "he will save his people from their sins" (Matt 1:21), the loose ends will be tied and the gaping hole will be filled. The one who will be Prophet, Priest, King, and even the sacrificial Lamb has arrived. He will stand in the gap left by the resounding failures of the Old Testament. He will fulfill the prophecies spoken by the prophets hundreds of years earlier. He will reveal the Father. The fulfillment of the promise in Genesis 3:15 will be met in Jesus: He will crush the head of the serpent.

The Gospel writer Luke gives us the most details and helps us connect the events of Jesus' birth and life to several Old Testament prophecies:

> But the angel said to her, "Do not be afraid, Mary, you have found favor with God. You will be with child and give birth to a son, and you are to give him the name Jesus. He will be great and will be called the Son of the Most High. The Lord God will give him the throne of his father David, and he will reign over the house of Jacob forever; his kingdom will never end." (Luke 1:30–33)

Luke makes it clear in the full account of Jesus' birth that Mary, the young girl engaged to Joseph, became pregnant without losing her virginity. Hundreds of years earlier, the prophet Isaiah spoke of this:

> "Therefore the Lord himself will give you a sign: The virgin will be with child and will give birth to a son, and will call him Immanuel. . . . For to us a child is born, to us a son is given, and the government will be on his shoulders. And he will be called Wonderful Counselor, Mighty God, Everlasting Father, Prince of Peace. Of the increase of his government and peace there will be no end. He will reign on David's throne and over his kingdom, establishing and upholding it with justice and righteousness from that time on and forever. The zeal of the Lord Almighty will accomplish this." (Isa 7:14; 9:6–7)

The conception of Jesus by a special creative act of God the Father and God the Holy Spirit means that Jesus was born free of the guilt and depravity that plagues and ultimately condemns every human being. He was divine—totally God. Yet, born of Mary's flesh, He was also totally human. As a perfect human being, the first (and last) since Adam, Jesus alone was qualified to represent humanity before God and become the perfect sacrifice for sin.

Luke's historical references to Jacob and David establish Jesus' credentials as a Jew and as a member of the royal line. Jacob was the grandson of Abraham, the father of the Jewish people, to whom God had promised personal blessings and blessings to all peoples on the earth (Gen 12:1–3). The promise was repeated to Isaac, and then to his son Jacob. Jacob's twelve sons became the progenitors of the twelve tribes of Israel, and the promise passed to Jacob's son Judah: "The scepter will not depart from Judah, nor the ruler's staff from between his feet, until he comes to whom it belongs and the obedience of the nations is his" (Gen 49:10). The birth of Jesus, announced first to lowly Jewish shepherds and then extending to Persian kings, set the stage for the blessing of the whole earth, just as God had promised Abraham so many years earlier. All levels of society and every race of people were included. In Jesus' relationship to David, we see another aspect of who He was. David was the second king of Israel. God's favor rested on him, and He promised him an everlasting dynasty (2 Sam 7:11b–16). Until the exile of the people to Babylon, a Davidic descendant sat on the throne, but after the exile, the kingship was never reestablished. What happened to God's promise? Jesus came. From the tribe of Judah through Mary's husband, Joseph, Jesus was the final fulfillment of the promise to David. He is the one who will reign forever.

It is also in the New Testament that we learn Jesus has been involved in the affairs of the world since the very beginning. While God the Son did not take on human form until the first century AD, He has always existed as the second person of the Trinity. He existed with God the Father before time began, and the Apostle John tells us that He was instrumental in creation. The baby in the manger was the Creator of the world into which He was born: "In the beginning was the Word, and the Word was with God, and the Word was God. He was with God in the beginning. Through him all things were made; without him nothing was made that has been made. . . . The Word became flesh and made his dwelling among us" (John 1:1–3, 14).

Paul adds to this in Colossians when he speaks of Christ as Creator as well as Sustainer of the universe. Through His power He holds all of creation together: "He is the image of the invisible God, the firstborn over all creation. For by him all things were created: things in heaven and on earth, visible and invisible, whether thrones or powers or rulers or authorities; all things were created by him and for him. He is before all things, and in him all things hold together" (Col 1:15–17).

The Climax of the Story

The New Testament also shows us Jesus as the final, perfect sacrifice in the sacrificial system. Near the end of His ministry, Jesus told His disciples that He had come to serve, "and to give his life as a ransom for many" (Matt 20:28). Jesus, in His body on the cross, was the payment price to free us from the penalty due God for human sin; He was the ransom. The Apostle Paul tells us exactly what this ransom means:

> But now a righteousness from God, apart from law, has been made known, to which the Law and the Prophets testify. This righteousness from God comes through faith in Jesus Christ to all who believe. There is no difference, for all have sinned and fall short of the glory of God, and are justified freely by his grace through the redemption that came by Christ Jesus. God presented him as a sacrifice of atonement, through faith in his blood. (Rom 3:21–25)

Jesus endured the full wrath and abandonment of God during three hours of darkness on the cross. No wonder He echoed the words of Psalm 22:1 and cried, "My God, my God, why have you forsaken me?" (Matt 27:46). Isaiah had spoken of this crushing weight as well: "But he was pierced for our transgressions, he was crushed for our iniquities; the punishment that brought us peace was upon him, and by his wounds we are healed. We all, like sheep, have gone astray, each of us has turned to his own way; and the Lord has laid on him the iniquity of us all" Isa 53:5–6).

It is only because of this sacrifice that anybody can gain right standing with God. The sacrificial death of Jesus allowed God to vent His holy wrath on Jesus, fully satisfying the justice His holiness demanded. At the same time, God could, in a legal sense, acquit sinners who accepted Jesus' death as payment for all the charges against them. Jesus took the punishment. Furthermore, because Jesus lived a perfect human life, God can credit these same sinners with Jesus' righteousness. Paul emphasizes this in 2 Corinthians 5:21: "God made him who had no sin to be sin for us, so that in him we might become the righteousness of God." Peter Lewis explains it this way: "Christ suffered for our sins as though they were His own so that we might enjoy the reward of His righteousness as though that had been our own. By imputation we receive His perfect obedience in life even as He took our transgressions in death."[2]

But, Jesus' death is not the end of the story. He was buried and sealed in a tomb that was guarded by soldiers. Nonetheless, three days later the Lord Jesus Christ arose from the dead and left the tomb of His own accord. All four gospel writers relate the account as historical fact. The message later preached by the disciples—and their eventual deaths as martyrs—was rooted in the reality of the resurrection. The bodily resurrection of Jesus is

---

2. Peter Lewis, *The Glory of Christ*, 303.

the linchpin of the Christian faith. If Christ did not rise, Paul says, then Christians are, of all people, most miserable (1 Cor 15:16–19).

Why is the resurrection so important? For at least three reasons. First, Jesus said He would rise again; if He is credible (and if He is God), it had to happen as He said it would. Second, in His resurrection from the dead, Jesus defeated death; He was more powerful than Satan and his domain. Third, it is because Jesus arose from the dead and took on a new body that we have the same hope; He was the "firstfruits," meaning a full harvest is to follow. Because He defeated death, someday we will rise from the dead, receive glorified bodies that will never decay, and live forever with Him: we are the harvest to follow (1 Cor 15). Again, Lewis says, "Christ's resurrection signifies now and for all-time the redemption of man in the body, from sickness, pain, and death."[3] He goes on to talk about the struggles we have in our own bodies with pain, lusts, and weakness; we deal with these things on a daily basis for as long as we live. The resurrection of Jesus with a new and glorified body assures us that we too will someday be raised with a glorified body and freed from all the weaknesses of our sinful human bodies. This is our great hope.

Jesus' resurrection completed His work on earth. If He had just died, He would have been a dead sacrifice like so many that preceded Him. And we would still be held captive by sin and death. But because He rose from the dead, Jesus conquered our last and greatest enemy. He defeated death. Christ instituted a new order through His victory over death; He took away the fear of death and gave those who belong to Him the opportunity to understand death as the stepping-stone to an eternal life.

The End Is Just the Beginning

Then Jesus returned to heaven to carry on a new work there. First, He was crowned and given the nations as His inheritance (Ps 2). And then, seated at the Father's right hand, He began His heavenly work on behalf of all believers: He sent the Holy Spirit to indwell and empower the apostles and all believers (then and now), and He became the Great High Priest and Mediator between God and believers. He intercedes for His own before God when they sin. He is the Advocate.

And yet, the Story does not end even there. When Jesus ascended to heaven, angels told His disciples that He would return to earth again some day in just the same way He had left. At that time He will establish His eternal kingdom where He will reign with all whose names are in the Lamb's

3. Ibid., 371–72.

Book of Life forever. Those who have received, by faith, the gift of God's great salvation and who then lived to please Him, will receive a gloried body and will live forever with God in a place of joy and perfection—the new earth. Those whose names are not recorded in the Book of Life—those who have lived for themselves and for sinful pleasure—will be condemned to eternal punishment and cast into a lake of fire (Rev 20:11–15).

Before Jesus appears in the New Testament, His coming has been foretold through prophets and His earthly mission has been prefigured through the sacrificial system. His second coming is even present in the shadows of Old Testament kingship. When He comes, He fulfills all that the prophets have said and reveals God: Jesus is the climax of the Old Testament's storyline and He remains the central figure throughout the book of Revelation. Everything goes back to Him—then, now, and forever.

Through Jesus, God has answered the death question. But God does not automatically apply salvation to everyone the moment they are born. It is only granted to people through the unmerited favor of God. Through humble acknowledgement that we are unable to atone for our own sins and by faith in the efficacy of the atoning sacrifice of Jesus Christ, we receive salvation: "For it is by grace you have been saved, through faith—and this not from yourselves, it is the gift of God—not by works, so that no one can boast. For we are God's workmanship, created in Christ Jesus to do good works, which God prepared in advance for us to do" (Eph 2:8–10). There is no price put on God's gift of salvation, but there is an expectation that those who accept God's gift will devote the rest of their lives to living according to His program and doing the works for which God has equipped them and which will advance His kingdom in this world.

Ultimate Issues and School Subjects

God's plan competes in a world of many religions, philosophies, and theologies. You face the challenge of helping your students understand many of these, while also helping them understand what the New Testament teaches about encountering Jesus. At the elementary level, this teaching emerges most often in "teachable moments," not structured curriculum as in the upper grades.

Jesus is not merely a subject to be studied: He is a Person to be answered. In His conversation with a Pharisee named Nicodemus, Jesus said that no one can see the kingdom of God unless He is born again (John 3:3). He made it very clear that He came to bring life and salvation, not condemnation, but that faith is the key to salvation (John 3:16–17).

Philosophy—the Search for Wisdom

Leading your students to this realization and then prayerfully allowing God to finish the work is among your most important tasks.

Philosophy simply means the love or pursuit of wisdom. It deals with the big questions of life, like what is real? what does it mean to be human? what is truth? what is right and wrong? what is beauty? Everyone has answers of some kind for these questions: sometimes the answers come from personal contemplation, sometimes from the culture, sometimes from the educational system—and very often, they don't form a cohesive system of thought. For example, at a recent demonstration in Madison, Wisconsin (a place well known for its liberalism and tolerant plurality), scores of angry citizens protested a Nazi rally being held in the city, saying that Madison did not want Nazis. But most of the people who decried the presence of Nazis in one breath would have said in the next that everyone has the right to believe and practice as they see fit. People live "comfortably" with the inconsistencies in their philosophical belief systems.

In the proper study of philosophy, answers are found using reason, the ability to assess data, form conclusions, make judgments, and draw inferences from observation. Sometimes intuition—forming ideas internally, without an evaluation of external data—brings answers. Many philosophers depend on the individual and collective ability of the human mind to understand the world and provide answers to life's basic questions. But for Christians, answers also come through the revelation of God. By acknowledging that God has spoken and His words are true, these philosophers address issues in a larger arena of thought. They use the intellectual abilities given to them by God to think (reason) and they include God's thoughts (revelation) regarding life's basic issues.

Everyone is a philosopher in some respect: we all reach answers of some kind about life's big questions, and each philosopher operates with biases and assumptions. While some think they are approaching their task with wide-open minds, they are not. It is impossible to think without doing so through a worldview. The goal of teaching philosophy, formally and informally, in a Christian school is to help our students begin in the right place, recognize the thought processes happening around them, and evaluate ideas through the lenses of revelation and reason.

Religion and Theology—Who's in Charge Here?

Religions are all over the world. Most people have a religious system that holds great meaning for them and determines to some degree the conduct of their daily lives. The religions of the world have grown out of human recognition that there are forces or powers at work more powerful than people.[4] Some of these forces are responsible for what exists, others for the provision of daily needs, and yet others for the afterlife. Cultures named these powers and worshipped them as deities, seeking to appease or manipulate them for their own well-being. The attributes and behaviors of the deities mirror and exceed human attributes and behaviors—people project their own attributes and behaviors onto their gods as a way to understand them.

In the supposed sophistication of our age, many religions deny the presence and activity of the supernatural altogether. The adherents of these "religions" explain all the happenings in the world rationally, and they worship, if you will, human power. The highest power is human power and potential; there is nothing humanity cannot accomplish if it puts its minds and energies to it.

In the Christian worldview, the framework for understanding the world's religions comes from Romans 1 where Paul makes a stunning assertion: everyone knows that God exists, but many suppress this truth:

> The wrath of God is being revealed from heaven against all the godlessness and wickedness of men who suppress the truth by their wickedness, since what may be known about God is plain to them, because God has made it plain to them. For since the creation of the world God's invisible qualities—his eternal power and divine nature—have been clearly seen, being understood from what has been made, so that men are without excuse.
>
> For although they knew God, they neither glorified him as God nor gave thanks to him, but their thinking became futile and their foolish hearts were darkened. Although they claimed to be wise, they became fools and exchanged the glory of the immortal God for images made to look like mortal man and birds and animals and reptiles. (Rom 1:18–23)

Even an atheist *knows* that God exists. Any religion that denies God's revelation and thus man's standing before Him is an attempt to circumvent the Truth. The task of Christian school teachers is to teach our students

---

4. Even religions that eventually came into being based on the writings of one person (who sometimes claimed his or her words were special revelation) have the underlying belief that some power, given to their leader, supercedes the normal power of humanity.

to acknowledge the Truth, not suppress it as sinful humanity is prone to do. Only when our students understand their own sin and standing before God can they begin to understand what drives humanity to create gods in its own image.

Another aspect of teaching our students "religion" is incorporating church history into the curriculum. In the independent spirit of American culture, it is easy to overlook the fact that we stand on the shoulders of those who have gone before, but we and our students should know the basic story of Christianity from the early church to modern times. It is easy to forget that people like Augustine, Aquinas, Luther, Bunyan, Wesley, and Wilberforce lived and died with a devotion to purify, preserve, and advance the message of the church. Meeting them and coming to appreciate their contributions is part of our memory as a church. As our history, they anchor us to a tradition that extends back to the apostles, Jesus, and the Jewish roots of the Old Testament. We are part of that legacy.

Bible—Learning from the Ultimate Source

It is impossible to teach philosophy and religion "Christianly" without the Bible, but in the Christian school, we also teach the Bible on its own merits. In the primary grades, our students learn the major characters and stories: Adam and Eve, Noah and the ark, Abraham, David, Jesus, and Paul, to name a few. We teach them the books of the Bible, the Ten Commandments, the difference between the Old and New Testaments, and countless lessons that emerge from its pages. When our students reach middle school and high school, we help them learn how to study the Book for themselves, and we help them learn how to mine it for the answers they need to live rightly.

The Bible is unique among all our textbooks in that it alone is special revelation from God and thus not subject to change or modification. Absolute truth is not a popular idea in our culture, and neither is the historical accuracy and utter reliability of the Bible. As we nurture our students in the Book, we must help them think through the concept of "Truth" as it relates to God: if we just tell them what to believe about the Bible, they will not be equipped to face the onslaught of a culture (and its institutions of higher education) that long ago decided the Bible is obsolete. Helping your students realize the reliability and relevancy of the Bible is no small task, but it's not something you can just *tell* them. You will have to *show* them—through the enthusiasm and power with which you teach it, and by the integrity with which you live it. Don't ever bore your students with the most exciting, intriguing, timeless, relevant, life-saving Book in the world!

Conclusion

The story of Jesus—the *Person* of Jesus—is not like anything else you will teach. It demands more than responses on essay exams or multiple choice quizzes. Jesus Himself demands a response. This, unfortunately, is not something you can require of your students. Each person will answer Jesus in this lifetime or the next. The goal of your teaching, as we've already said, is to lead your students into a lifetime of rewarding relationship with Jesus. You want your students to learn how to live rightly, to respond personally to Jesus.

Summary of Truths

Answering the Big Questions

1. What we understand and believe about death affects how we live.
2. Only the Christian worldview can provide a coherent framework through which to understand life's big questions.
3. Jesus is the central person of all history, and according to the Bible, He can only be truly accepted as Lord.
4. What we believe about Jesus and how we respond to Him determines how we live and how we die.

Who Is Jesus?

1. The story of Jesus runs through the entire Bible.
2. The Gospels give us the account of Jesus' birth, ministry, death, resurrection, and ascension.
3. After His ascension, Jesus is present among His disciples and the early church in the person of the Holy Spirit.
4. The book of Revelation shows Jesus to be the Lamb slain who will judge all the earth.

Jesus in the Old Testament

1. While we meet Jesus "face-to-face" in the New Testament, the Old Testament prepares the way for Him, prophesies of Him, and prefigures Him in types.

    a. The perfectly created world was marred by Adam and Eve when they sinned, but almost immediately, God initiated a plan to redeem His creation by promising a Savior who would one day crush the power of Satan.
    b. God chose a group of people—the Jews—through whom to reveal Himself and ultimately to send the Savior.
    c. God's people were sinful and willfully disobeyed Him, and since God is a holy God, He cannot condone sin. He must punish it.
    d. Sinful human beings can only approach God if atonement has been made for their sins.
    e. God established a system of offerings and sacrifices for His people Israel so they would understand their sinfulness, God's holiness, and the need to bridge the gulf that sin created between them.
    f. Israel repeatedly offered the blood of unblemished animals as the atonement for their sins.
    g. This sacrificial system was a means of substitution whereby animals filled the place of punishment deserved by people.
    h. The priests who offered the sacrifices were sinners and some of them were corrupt, too. The sacrificial system ultimately fell short of saving people.
2. When the people demanded a king, God gave them one, but every king fell short of God's requirements for leaders. God promised that there would be a perfect king who would reign forever.
3. God sent prophets to warn His people about their sins and to urge them to repent. The prophets also told about the coming of a Messiah.

Jesus in the New Testament

1. When Jesus appears on the scene after the Old Testament paves the way for Him, He is the fulfillment of many prophecies.
    a. His mother was a descendent of the family of King David from the tribe of Judah of the family of Abraham.
    b. His mother conceived Him through an act of the Holy Spirit when she was engaged to be married to Joseph.
    c. Jesus' virginal conception allowed Him to be born human, yet without a sin nature.

2. In the New Testament, we also learn that Jesus was involved in the creation of the heavens and the earth and that He sustains all things.
3. Because He alone was perfect, Jesus was the only one who could be a final and sufficient sacrifice for sins. He endured God's judgment so we could be forgiven and His righteousness could be credited to us.
4. Jesus' death followed the Old Testament pattern in which Jesus became the substitute offering in place of human beings. He was the final offering.
5. Jesus death was the worst kind of death that could be inflicted on a person, the most agonizing way to die. In it He endured the full wrath of God against sin.
6. Jesus' death and resurrection were the fulfillment of God's promise of a Savior given in the garden of Eden.
7. The resurrection of Jesus from the dead is the linchpin of the Christian faith.
    a. When He was resurrected, Jesus fulfilled His own prophecies.
    b. His mission to redeem sinners would have been a failure without the resurrection; He would simply have been another dead sacrifice like so many (animals) before.
    c. It demonstrated His victory over death and sin, and it is the substance of our hope of victory over death.
    d. Because Jesus was raised from the dead, we can be assured that we, too, will rise from the dead some day.
8. When Jesus ascended to the Father's right hand in heaven, He completed His mission of redemption, and He began two important activities on our behalf.
    a. He sent the Holy Spirit to empower His followers to take the gospel to the world.
    b. He intercedes before God on our behalf; He is our advocate when we are tested and tempted by Satan.
9. All who through faith receive His saving grace become new creatures in Christ and have their names entered into the Book of Life.
10. Jesus has promised to return, and when He does, He will judge the righteous and the unrighteous.
    a. The unrighteous, whose names are not in the Book of Life, will be cast into the lake of fire where they will be forever.
    b. The righteous, whose names are in the Book of Life, will live forever with God on the new earth.
11. Jesus has answered the issue of death by overcoming death through His resurrection. There is life beyond the grave.

Ultimate Issues and School Subjects

1. Philosophy represents deep human thinking on the big issues of life. Everyone is a "philosopher," but we differ in our sources of knowledge.
    a. Some people rely entirely on human thinking (reason).
    b. Some people also rely on what God has to say about things (revelation).
2. Religions and theologies developed from human understanding that there are forces in the universe that are greater than us.
    a. Humans developed gods, gave them attributes and powers, and then worshiped, appeased, and feared them.
    b. Even people who claim not to believe in God or gods have a god—the human being or the human ability to reason.
3. The Bible, God's revelation of Himself, should lie behind everything we teach as Christian teachers, but in Christian schools, we also study *it* as the inspired Word of God.

Teaching Tips

1. Look Who's Talking. Bring in a collection of television ads and play them for the students. Then play them again, one by one, and discuss the worldviews and philosophies at work behind them. Discuss the philosophy behind modern marketing and how they accord with biblical principles. Discuss what the objectives of Christian "marketing" should be. How should the two look different? Do they? Can your students think of examples? (Junior high and high school)

2. At the Center of Everything. Make several copies of a picture of a cross and post it all over your classroom and even around the school, if possible. Don't tell your students why you've put them there; leave them there for a day or two. Then ask the students why they think you've put the pictures up. Talk about what it means for Jesus to be the most important thing in our lives. He is everywhere we go, and He should be in our mind no matter what we are doing. Talk about how we might do things differently if we remembered this about Jesus. (Primary grades)

3. Who Do You Say I Am? Have students bring in cultural ideas of Jesus found on television, in movies, on the Internet, and wherever else they come across them. (Be careful as some may be blasphemous.) Bring in some examples yourself. Examine each idea and have the class determine what the people think of Jesus. Why might they think

this way? Compare these ideas to the Bible. (Upper elementary and junior high)

4. The Bible in Real Time. Have the students assemble a massive timeline for a classroom wall. Divide them into smaller groups and assign them sections. Have them chart the major events of the Bible, as well as marking the books where they fall. Also incorporate other world events on your timeline so the students can see where the Bible's times fall in terms of other historical events. (Upper elementary, junior high, and high school)

5. Standing on Their Shoulders. Each generation adds to the learning of previous generations (we "stand on their shoulders"), and it is important for our students to appreciate the history that leads to present-day disciplines. Compile a list of Christians who have worked in your subject area, and as part of your semester's assigned workload, have students read a biography of a Christian in your field and report in writing or to the class what the person accomplished, how faith influenced his or her studies, and what legacy he or she has left. (Junior high and high school)

Additional Resources

1. Colson, Charles, and Nancy Pearcey. *How Now Should We Live?* Wheaton: Tyndale House, 1999. The goal of this best-selling book is to help Christians understand biblical faith as an entire worldview, and thus to be able to engage in the struggle between competing worldviews in our culture.

2. Donovan, Vincent J. *Christianity Rediscovered.* Maryknoll, NY: Orbis, 2001. Written by a Catholic priest in an African missionary context, this provocative book offers much for Christians in post-modern America to think about related to missions and the gospel message.

3. Martens, Elmer A. *God's Design: A Focus on Old Testament Theology.* 3d ed. N. Richland Hills, TX: BIBAL Press, 1998. Most Christians know more about the New Testament than the Old, and this book provides a helpful grid through which to read and understand the Old Testament message.

4. Moreland, J. P. *Love Your God with All Your Mind: The Role of Reason in the Life of the Soul.* Colorado Springs: NavPress, 1997. Moreland confronts the decline of Christian thinking, challenging and instructing Christians how to develop a mature mind in service of the kingdom of God—through evangelism, apologetics, worship, and vocation.

5. Noll, Mark A. *The Scandal of the Evangelical Mind.* Grand Rapids: Eerdmans, 1994. "The scandal of the evangelical mind is that there is not much of an evangelical mind," begins Noll in this compelling call to serious intellectual life in the evangelical community.

6. Pearcey, Nancy. *Total Truth: Liberating Christianity from Its Cultural Captivity.* Wheaton: Crossway Books, 2004. A must-read for every Christian, this book clearly traces the path Western Christianity has followed for the past few centuries. Pearcey is a fantastically clear writer in her explanation of how Christians should think and live differently in the world. She makes application to the social and biological sciences.

7. Poe, Harry Lee. *See No Evil: The Existence of Sin in a World of Relativism.* Grand Rapids: Kregel Publications, 2004. Poe provides an articulate look at sin and evil, defining sin in terms of a broken relationship rather than violation of all absolutes. This shaping of the gospel story finds ready inroads in today's post-modern mind.

8. Schaeffer, Francis A. *How Should We Then Live? The Rise and Decline of Western Thought and Culture.* Old Tappan, NJ: Fleming H. Revell, 1976. Schaeffer's book is a classic, offering an analysis of key moments in history that have shaped modern culture, as well as the philosophies behind these moments. His goal is to offer solutions for the future based on knowledge of the past.

9. Sire, James W. *The Universe Next Door: A Basic Worldview Catalog.* 3d ed. Downers Grove, IL: InterVarsity Press, 1997. The oft-cited worldview primer, Sire's book surveys the smorgasbord of worldviews from deism to nihilism to post-modernism. It is a must for a Christian teacher's library.

10. Wittmer, Michael E. *Heaven Is a Place on Earth: Why Everything You Do Matters to God.* Grand Rapids: Zondervan, 2004. This book demonstrates the biblical case for the value of creation and redemption, which together supply the foundational motivation for every aspect of the Christian life.

Conclusion

WE HOPE by now you've gained (or regained) your view of the forest and are better equipped to integrate a biblical worldview across the curriculum you teach. It is hard work and it is never done. It is our sincerest desire that you commit to this task and do it with all your heart.

To help you begin the practical work of integrating a biblical worldview in your subjects, we've included here an edited version of an exercise professors underwent at a Christian college recently, as they put serious effort into cross-curricular integration. Obviously, you are teaching at a different level, but the process is the same. The exercise begins with a statement of the philosophy behind the integration and concludes with a worksheet that can be applied to each subject taught. We have concluded with a final list of resources that do not relate to specific disciplines but address important worldview issues.

The Commitment

We are committed to a Christian worldview that follows the contour of the biblical narrative. The Scriptures begin with the story of creation, a story that reminds us that this earth is a good place to be. God created a world so impressive that it satisfied His own impeccable standards. "It is good," He said. "It is very good."

Because creation is the good work of God, we are not only permitted but we are encouraged to enjoy it just as it is. We do not need to baptize the things of this world to make them suitable for Christian consumption. "Everything God created is good," Paul writes, and "nothing is to be rejected if it is received with thanksgiving . . ." (1 Tim 4:4). God is pleased when His children thoroughly enjoy this beautiful creation that He has given to them. He wants us to celebrate, even indulge, in its goodness wherever we find it.

But God not only wants us to enjoy this world, He also commands us to take care of it (Gen 1:28; 2:15). He calls us to participate in His ongoing work of creation, developing the raw materials of the earth for maximum benefit. This command to create culture gives spiritual significance to every human task. Whether we are caring for children, studying for a test, punching a time clock, mowing the lawn, chasing a fly ball, shopping for groceries, following a diet, or brushing our teeth, it all qualifies as obedience to the cultural mandate, and as such should be done "with all your heart, as working for the Lord, not for men" (Col 3:23).

Unfortunately, this opening movement of creation is not the end of the story. We learn from the story of the fall that something has gone terribly wrong. Things are not the way they are supposed to be in the world. When Adam chose to reject God's Word and foolishly live as he pleased, his rebellion contaminated every last corner of creation.

Because of this universal presence of sin, Christians must now balance enjoyment of this world with a healthy fear of the evil that lurks there. A video that inspires may also include scenes that sear our conscience. A pleasing melody may carry lyrics that soil the soul. An engaging story might subtly stoke the flames of lust. We must guard our hearts as we live in this sinful age, ready to flee at the first sign of temptation so that we might become holy children of our heavenly Father.

However, though we must run from the world's temptations we must not run from the world itself. The final movement in the biblical story records God's plan to redeem His creation. Here God calls us to join His efforts to turn back evil and establish righteousness in every aspect of culture. We believe it is our Christian duty to examine every facet of culture from this biblical perspective. We run every discipline through the grid of creation, fall, and redemption. We ask, "What created goodness is present?" "What fallen aspects are here?" and "How might we reclaim this area for the glory of God?" Besides seeking to redeem each area of God's world, we also seek to integrate across the disciplines. Because God's world is a unity, a comprehensive worldview must strive to understand how each part of God's world interrelates with every other area.[1]

The Process

With this statement in mind, you can work through the following questions:

1. Think about your discipline in the abstract.

---

1. Thanks to Mike Wittmer for sharing this material that he created and used at Cornerstone University, Grand Rapids, Michigan. The questions to follow are also his material.

a. Creation:
      i. How does your discipline fit into God's world? What role does it play in our school?
      ii. How does your discipline interrelate with other areas? Think integration.
   b. Redemption: How does your discipline overcome the effects of sin and contribute to the well-being that God intended for this world?
2. Think about how your discipline is typically taught or lived in the real world.
   a. Fall:
      i. How has your discipline been misused by its practitioners?
      ii. How might your secular counterparts teach this discipline in ways that are not biblical, Christian, or right?
      iii. In what ways do people in the "real world" abuse your discipline?
3. Redemption: How can the way we teach or apply your discipline in this school correct the errors made in other places and restore the discipline to what God intended?

Additional Resources

1. Claerbaut, David. *Faith and Learning on the Edge*. Grand Rapids: Zondervan, 2004. Claerbaut calls Christian educators to resist pagan thinking in their disciplines and then shows how to do it in various disciplines.

2. Plantinga, Cornelius, Jr. *Engaging God's World: A Christian Vision of Faith, Learning, and Living*. Grand Rapids: Eerdmans, 2002. This is a beautifully written and inspiring book on the value and method of Christian education. Plantinga, president of Calvin Seminary, wrote the book for college freshmen and it is a wonderful introduction to worldview.

3. Wolters, Albert M. *Creation Regained: Biblical Basics for a Reformational Worldview*. 2d ed. Grand Rapids: Eerdmans, 2005. Wolters supplies the creation-fall-redemption grid which must govern all of the Christian life, and in our context, Christian education. He talks about the structure of things as God created them, and the direction things have taken after the fall.

Bibliography

Augustine. *City of God.* Translated by Gerald G. Walsh, et al. New York: Image Books, 1958.

Calvin, John. *The Institutes of the Christian Religion.* Translated by Henry Beveridge. Grand Rapids: Eerdmans, 1989.

Colson, Charles, and Nancy Pearcey. *How Now Shall We Live?* Wheaton: Tyndale House, 1999.

Crawford, Albert "Joe." "Systematic Theology 1 (A Second Draft)" (class notes for Grand Rapids Theological Seminary, 1999).

Davies, Paul. *The Mind of God.* New York: Simon & Schuster, 1992.

Fee, Gordon D., and Douglas Stuart. *How to Read the Bible for All Its Worth.* Grand Rapids: Zondervan, 1981, 1993.

Forbes, Cheryl. *Imagination: Embracing a Theology of Wonder.* Portland, OR: Multnomah Press, 1986.

Gaebelein, Frank E. *The Christian, the Arts, and Truth: Regaining the Vision of Greatness.* Compiled by D. Bruce Lockerbie. Portland, OR: Multnomah Press, 1985.

Grier, James. *The Ten Words: Moral Choices Begin with the Ten Commandments,* audiotapes of ten lectures. Grand Rapids: Cornerstone Audio Services, 2000.

Hoekema, Anthony A. *Created in God's Image.* Grand Rapids: Eerdmans, 1986.

Johnstone, Patrick, and Jason Mandryk. *Operation World: 21st Century Edition.* 6th ed. Waynesboro, GA: Paternoster, 2001.

Keller, Helen H. *Helen Keller: The Story of My Life.* New York: Airmont, 1965.

Lewis, C. S. *Mere Christianity.* New York: The MacMillan Company, 1960.

Lewis, Peter. *The Glory of Christ.* Chicago: Moody Press, 1997.

Ryken, Leland. *Culture in Christian Perspective: A Door to Understanding & Enjoying the Arts.* Portland, OR: Multnomah Press, 1986.

———. *How to Read the Bible as Literature.* Grand Rapids: Zondervan, 1984.

———. *Windows to the World: Literature in Christian Perspective.* Grand Rapids: Zondervan, 1985.

Sproul, R. C. *Lifeviews: Making a Christian Impact on Culture and Society.* Grand Rapids: Fleming Revell, 1986.

Tomasino, Anthony J. *Written Upon the Heart: The Ten Commandments for Today's Christian.* Grand Rapids: Kregel Publications, 2001.

Watt, Ward B. "Insects." In *World Book Encyclopedia* 10:278–301. Chicago: World Book, 2000.

Widder, Wendy. *A Match Made in Heaven: How Singles and the Church Can Live Happily Ever After.* Grand Rapids: Kregel Publications, 2003.

———. "'Twas the Night of the Program." *Teachers in Focus* 5 (1996/1997), 16.

Winner, Lauren F. *Girl Meets God: On the Path to a Spiritual Life*. Chapel Hill: Algonquin Books of Chapel Hill, 2002.

Wittmer, Michael E. *Heaven Is a Place on Earth: Why Everything You Do Matters to God*. Grand Rapids: Zondervan, 2004.

Wolterstorff, Nicholas. *Art in Action*. Grand Rapids: Eerdmans, 1980.

Yancey, Philip. *The Bible Jesus Read*. Grand Rapids: Zondervan, 1999.

———. *Where is God When It Hurts?* Grand Rapids: Zondervan, 1990.

www.ingramcontent.com/pod-product-compliance
Lightning Source LLC
Chambersburg PA
CBHW071437160426
43195CB00013B/1932